MUST OUR SCHOOLS DIE?

DAVID H. PAYNTER

MULTNOMAH PRESS
Portland, Oregon 97266

Cover design by Britt Taylor Collins

MUST OUR SCHOOLS DIE?
©1980 by Multnomah Press
Portland, Oregon 97266

Printed in the United States of America

First Printing, 1980

Library of Congress Cataloging in Publication Data

Paynter, David H
    Must our schools die?

    Includes index.
    1,   Public schools—United States.   I.   Title.
LA217.P39   1980   371'.01'0973   80-23368
ISBN 0-930014-44-8
ISBN 0-930014-53-7 (pbk.)

Preface

The multi-pronged advancement of society in the first eighty years of the twentieth century has forced thoughtful educators to look closely at the future of public schools and the challenges through the year 2000. But we cannot dawdle through this time. A revolutionary alteration in public instruction is an immediate necessity. Significant changes must be implemented as soon as possible.

My proposals for change may be considered radical by traditionalists, yet nothing short of a complete departure from tradition can correct the problems. The public schools must return to the citizens their legitimate role in decision-making processes.

The writing of a book about total educational reform is a dangerous project. Why? In the first place, new methods and changes in education open the door for the innovator in education who seeks change for "change's sake" alone. Change is proposed in individual areas thus segmenting education. Desperately needed are proposals for *overall* reform that provide a consistent pattern of education for the students in our schools.

There is yet another danger, possibly more severe in its effect on improved education.

The present, accepted patterns of education have become towers of security and comfort for many educators. History shows us that these educators who sit comfortably in the security of the past fail to take into account the requirements of the present.

This second danger poses a real hindrance to an objective reading of this book. The educator who stoically holds to traditional methods without considering the needs of the future will react according to defense mechanisms when considering the reforms presented. Individuals in this category will tend to consider the reforms from an emotional position rather than reviewing them with a vision toward improvement.

The author urges those who may find themselves at either one of these danger points to approach the text recognizing the inherent problems in educational extremism. Unless representatives of these positions are willing to be guided by an objective examination of the needs of young people today, the success of any proposed educational reform is doomed to failure.

My proposals will lead to a complete break from the past and its failures. But these same proposals are built upon the successes of the past with the further understanding that if our school system is to survive, there must be a unified, clear plan for its future. We must first, then, explain the historical foundation for the patterns of the past in order that we might fully recognize the needs and plan for the future.

Readers should readily understand that a set of blueprints to revitalize a withered process is not produced completely by one mind. Many colleagues have participated in the development of the reforms proposed and a wealth of experience and observation has been the catalyst to the author. To my colleagues and professional associates of the past, the author is truly grateful.

PREFACE

I wish to acknowledge my deep indebtedness to the following persons for the help they have given: (1) my wife, Beverly, for her assistance and patience during the preparation of the manuscript; (2) the professional educators with whom I have had the opportunity of serving and who have stimulated my thinking and challenged me to seek ways of improving education; (3) my close friends with whom I have worked in discussing proposed reforms and the direction of education. To these people I extend a special note of deep appreciation

David H. Paynter
Garden Grove, California

Contents

Introduction 11

Part 1: The American Education Heritage
   Chapter 1 — Our Schooling Begins 17
   Chapter 2 — So Says the Law 23
   Chapter 3 — The Random Institution 29
   Chapter 4 — Local Control — Going, Going, Gone? . 37
   Chapter 5 — The Tax Dollar 43
   Chapter 6 — Why Schools Change 49
   Chapter 7 — A Tour of the Battlegrounds 63

PART 2: Death Knell for the Public Schools
   Chapter 8 — Crime and Punishment 79
   Chapter 9 — Equal Opportunity and Finances 93
   Chapter 10 — The Battle Is Joined 97
   Chapter 11 — The Community Can Win 109

PART 3: Twelve Reforms
   Chapter 12 — Eye on the Local Citizen 117
   Chapter 13 — Three R's Foundation Program 125
   Chapter 14 — Taking It to the Teachers 143
   Chapter 15 — The World After the Sixth Grade 151

CONTENTS

PART 3: Twelve Reforms (Continued)

   Chapter 16 — Education As You Like It 159

   Chapter 17 — Freedom to Learn 167

   Chapter 18 — Name Your Goal 177

   Chapter 19 — Help Always at Hand 183

   Chapter 20 — Fiscal Planning — Finally 189

   Chapter 21 — Committee Called to Account 195

   Chapter 22 — Finance Index Tells All 201

   Chapter 23 — The State at Local Level 205

Afterword 215

Subject Index 219

Introduction

No one needs to tell the educator today that our system is in serious difficulty.

We read it over and over again in newspapers, periodicals, and almost any publication dealing with education. *The Los Angeles Times* in an article in the Sunday edition, August 28, 1977, reported that "Last week the college entrance examination board announced that freshmen entering American colleges this fall received, on the average, the lowest scores on the scholastic aptitude test (SAT) ever recorded in the 51 years that it has been administered." The article further went on to state that a panel of twenty-one educators, foundation officials, and other experts headed by former Secretary of Labor Willard Werts had concurrently released the results of a major national study of declining academic achievement. The panel blamed the drop in student performance as measured by such tests as the SAT largely on an erosion of academic standards in the nation's high schools.

This article and others found in almost every publication clearly state the need for change. It is apparent that everyone is in agreement that there is a need for improvement, but few are prepared to present a blueprint for reform which puts together a planned program—a program which considers the health of the total educational system when presenting individual reforms. The pages of this book attempt to put together the past and examine the educational practices of today. Twelve detailed reforms for the future are then proposed.

It has been reported that there are 1,100 organizations concerned about the educational development of our people. We are indeed a nation of joiners. Of 192 of these organizations which were examined, it was found that 19 million members were reported. This figure includes people from all walks of life who in some way sought improvement individually or nationally for the development of our country's educational endeavor.

This indication of the segmentation of our society into separate interest areas is an example of the educational society itself. It is also an illustration as to why we find so many individual and innovative changes proposed for the educational system. These changes and innovations in themselves are initiated with the finest of motives yet often with little plan for how the innovator's change would affect the total education of the individual student. It is as though a doctor had determined that a replacement of an organ was essential for the well-being and health of the individual. It must be remembered, however, that when the operation is initiated, a plan for the recovery and future health of the individual must also be undertaken. This has not been the case when educational changes and innovations have been placed into the mainstream of the system of education *without* consideration of the effect on the health of the educational system.

Past efforts in education must be recognized. The reasons for the development of education to its position need to be considered. A plan of reform providing for the needs of the individuals and the requirements of our society has to be formulated. That is the plan of this book.

I recognize that no individual author would be allowed —let alone would have the ability—to establish a total plan for education without critical examination on the part of knowledgeable, practicing educators in today's profession. Any proposed plan of reform must bear the scrutiny and examination of those who are immediately involved in initiating the reform. Such scrutiny and examination are welcomed and sought by the writer in an effort to bring about the necessary improvement of education which is essential if it is to survive in the future.

Education can no longer benefit from individual innovations which fail to provide for continuity in the education process. Reform must take on a total plan recognizing the totality of education in order to effectively benefit the educational system. Education today is trapped by society and its extreme positions. No longer is there a basic body of truth accepted by people in general which permits the educational system to build upon a foundation accepted by the majority of the people. This foundation today is divided into those who support free enterprise, those who support a socialistic order, those who support the right, those who support the left. Those diversities in society present a unique task to the educator who seeks to provide a program for today.

Herein you will find a description of American education both good and bad. I will present bold steps of reform and renewal for the future and the rebirth of our schools. My plan of reform recognizes the crisis in education today and the diversity in our society. It is my hope that it also presents a blueprint for a coordinated program for total educational reform.

Part 1

The American Educational Heritage

1

Our Schooling Begins

Any discussion leading to revolution and new life for the public school system must be based on an understanding of the historical ups and downs in education, for the current system originates in colonial times.

The first step towards public education was taken by Puritan settlers in Massachusetts Bay Colony. Their Act, passed in 1642 by the General Court, was most remarkable. It was the first law in the new world to compel the teaching of reading and writing. The motive was religious instruction, but settlers soon realized that reading ability provided a means for understanding civil functions.

The law removed responsibility for the teaching of religious precepts from the home to the school. The Bible was established as the prime subject. The basic aim was to unfold the divine commands on which strict obedience in all walks of life was based. Original education stressed the three R's of colonial times: reading, writing, and religion.

The concept of fundamental education, revolving around a basic and limited curriculum, is not new. It can be dated from the earliest history of formal schooling. It reached its peak during the Middle Ages when the curriculum was restricted to the trivium of grammar, rhetoric, and logic. The incidental learnings known as the "quadrivium" were composed of arithmetic, music, geometry, and astronomy, and as a unit became the forerunner of modern sciences. With slight variation the founding fathers of this nation were products of this type of fundamental education, and with few revisions, this basic curricula determined the school program well into the twentieth century.

A goal of the Puritan schools was to insure that every person became a productive member of society. In 1644, the General Court held that parents and schoolmaster were responsible for both religious and vocational aims. Schooling was founded upon the practical concerns of knowledge and production: education for the good of the community. The legal concept of educational accountability was firmly established by our nation's forefathers.

Because parents were lax about sending their children to school, a second law was signed in 1647. It has been called the *Old Deluder Act.* It demanded that

> . . . every township of fifty householders shall forthwith appoint one person within their town to teach all children. . . to read and write, whose wages shall be paid by the parents and the inhabitants in general. . . When any town shall increase in numbers to one hundred families, they shall set up a grammar school, to instruct youth, so they may be fitted for the university. . . [and] if any town neglect their performance such town shall pay five pounds [each year] until this order shall be performed . . .

The early schools in Massachusetts, both public and private in operation and support, were financed by compulsory levies and tuition fees; funds were allocated from the General Court and supplemented by land grants or building subsidies to local communities.

Most schools were controlled by town selectmen. Later, the management came under the authority of the town council. It was the council's responsibility to choose the schoolmaster. Ministers often approved the appointments and inspected the programs, the church and local government working in tandem.

From the Puritans came twin concepts: the school was designed to shape the pupil's ability to read and write and to control his personal behavior so that he became productive. In accord with prevailing moral thought, school was to train the individual for his society.

As initial attempts to establish a system of education, early laws were milestones in school legislation. But the laws proved impossible to enforce. Many towns preferred to pay fines rather than set up grammar schools. Successive laws passed in 1671, 1701 and 1719 all increased the penalties. But colonialists apparently had yet to be convinced that public education should be controlled by those outside their local communities.

By the close of the colonial era, schools still had only the facade of an organized system. In reality, ever fearful of central control, separate groups in isolated communities still closely regulated them.

During the next one hundred and fifty years, schooling was mostly provided by private or religious organizations. Widely scattered and few in number, such schools were highly selective and open only to students of the leading families. Their operation and control rested with individuals or church boards.

The District is Born

During the entire colonial period, school management was carried out by a direct extension of the local government. As the towns grew and distances increased, children were unable to get to school. Consequently, schools were built in different places located throughout communities, and the first district system of control came into being. Colonial laws encouraged the formation of such local districts. The legislative intent was simple, the organization appealing. Any group of citizens could establish a school and impose taxes for its support. A community unwilling to enact taxation for schooling could retain a system of selective and private education.

From the outset, Americans have sought an active voice in their government's function. We have insisted that the "means of education" shall forever be encouraged, as set forth in the Continental Congress and later affirmed by the provisions of the *Northwest Ordinance* of 1787. But with or without encouragement, growth of public education was gradual and without thoughtful plan on any level. Since the Constitution left the process of education to the respective states, and they, in turn, referred schooling to local communities, the public school system developed without cohesive design or uniformity.

Education was a local responsibility, later to come under the aegis of the state. Though girded by national support, its main thrust was local.

The post-Revolutionary War period brought a growing demand for expansion of public education. In 1802, Thomas Jefferson proposed a system of free public elementary schools for the Commonwealth of Virginia. Although his efforts went unheeded, support for public education grew. In Massachusetts, under the leadership of Horace Mann, and later in Connecticut, following the efforts of Henry Barnard, the public school movement took root. Throughout the nineteenth century, states established more and more public schools and passed laws to raise funds for their operation. The small district pattern, slightly modified by city or county units of governing bodies, flourished into the twentieth century as the predominant organization for public schools.

Massachusetts, by a law enacted in 1827, established the first school board as a separate entity of the local government. Other states followed this action. School control became distinct from overall local government. Today, most states operate their public schools through local, city, or county boards of education. In California, for example, laws relating to the establishment, maintenance, government, and operation of public schools reside in the State Education Code.

In American democracy the state and its public school system have a crucial, working interrelationship. Schools not only exert influence, but influences, formal and informal, obvious and subtle, are exerted upon them. Today, people rely on the local school boards to resist any encroachment by state and federal governments.

The local school district remains a unique example of the layer-like governmental process. It is perhaps the local voter's last stronghold where he still exercises emotional control.

2

So Says the Law

Administration and management of the public schools may imply legal, quasi-legal, or political control. Each of the fifty states administers its public schools through a formidable body of legislative statutes. American education is ever in restrictive legal harness whenever the law is applied to the local community. School law cuts across the various divisions of civil law. It is rooted in constitutional requirements, legislative enactments, and judicial decisions at both the state and national levels of government. Each is a form of control over the legal authority vested in local boards. For example, a local board of education controls its expenditures only as permitted by law. A board may employ only teachers who possess valid credentials issued by a state agency acting under authority granted to it by some statute.

The 10th Amendment to the Constitution reserves to the respective states and to the people those powers neither delegated to the national government nor prohibited by it to the states. Education is the primary responsibility of the separate states. Today, the law declares that all children must attend school until they reach a specified age. Education is a legal duty of citizenship rather than an inherent right.

Since free education in America is a state function, the people create their own systems under separate consitutions. But the legal control of public education also is affected by the national government. Although the Constitution contains no specific reference to education, its general welfare clause has been interpreted broadly enough to permit passage of numerous congressional laws. Various other amendments have come before the U.S. Supreme Court for major decisions that affect public education. In addition, public schools are controlled by administrative regulations emanating from the executive branch of the federal government.

Attend and Support

The operation of any system of public schools is directly dependent upon compulsory attendance laws and tax support. Both demands are deeply imbedded in the constitutions and laws of several states. Originating with Massachusetts in 1843, and extending to Alaska and Hawaii today, each of the states has enacted compulsory attendance laws. Within such legislative controls, the states have preempted parental determination of school attendance. Early laws requiring tax support for the schools were permissive in nature. As schools were opened for the poor, money for their support became the strict legal responsibility of local communities. New York, in 1812, was the first state to enact a tax law. New Jersey, in 1828, passed a law to provide education for all children. By 1835, several more states had authorized general tax laws to support the schools.

The modern phrase, "education for all American youth," can be traced to our ancestors. It was the colonies' concept that education should be universal. Perhaps the most startling feature of early educational foundations was that schooling included public training that extended well into the teen years of both boys and girls. In 1853, New York enacted a Free School Law. One year later, Pennsylvania passed a general law establishing a system of graded public schools. Each of these statutes was based on compulsory attendance and tax support for secondary education. The *Kalamazoo (Michigan) Case,* decided by the Supreme Court in 1874, upheld the legality of the high school. Successive cases brought similar decisions in other states; all reaffirmed the principle of free, compulsory, and tax-supported secondary education.

Once the courts had clarified the fact that school boards of education possessed legal authority to establish schools and levels of instruction, the system was confronted with efforts to eliminate all nonpublic schools. In the *Oregon Case,* the Supreme Court in 1925 upheld the right of parents to control the type of education they wished for their offspring. The principle of alternate or religious schools was established. Successive decisions have affirmed the concept of separation of church and state.

Public and nonpublic schools have evolved in response to ideological, sociological, political, and practical demands of people. Their control remains a matter of major consequence. The fact that it continues to reside in the hands of local voters to some degree violates no constitutional precepts. Tax support, required attendance, and equal opportunity are the cornerstones of the American system of schools. But to millions, this triple concept reflects the growing power of government over church, home, and parent.

Teachers and the Law

Certain rights and responsibilities of those who teach are now established by statute. Contract employees within any public school system in any of the fifty states are required to possess valid certificates. Law also determines the procedures for issuance and revocation of such credentials or "certification."

Candidates for school positions who do not possess the necessary papers may not be employed by local boards of education.

Tenure is a teacher's job guarantee. After a satisfactory probation of from three to five years, permanent status—or tenure—is awarded. Although the tenured employee may be transferred within the system from one school to another or from one position to another, he or she generally is protected against reduction in salary or demotion in rank. But school systems cannot be required to maintain positions just to create jobs for the tenured. If unacceptable behavior is alleged, state laws usually entitle a tenured employee to an official notice, a statement of charges, and a hearing prior to any dismissal. Most statutes include incompetency, neglect of duty, unprofessional conduct, moral turpitude, and physical disability as reasons for dismissal.

Tenure laws have been met with varying emotion by both the public and the teacher. They have been frequent objects of litigation, but the right of the legislatures to change them has never been denied. Public education is thus under constant legal control.

An important aspect of a teacher's role is that the teacher stands *in loco parentis*. During school hours, he or she replaces the parent in the care and supervision of the student. As he or she can reward, so can he or she also punish. They have the legal right to corporal punishment as well as being responsible for the physical well-being of pupils.

But states have taken steps to counter possible abuse of the Puritan concept of control by cane, rod, and hickory stick. Most states have enacted laws that permit corporal punishment with qualifications. Punishment may not be "excessive," and must be suitable to the age and sex of the student. Its administration, following proper judgment, must be in good faith. Professional practice requires that the pupil clearly understands the reason for punishment. As long as corporal punishment is permitted, it must be carried out within the law.

In recent years, the broad usage of *in loco parentis* has gotten many a parent's ire up. Public school teachers, principals, and even local school boards have been sued for inflicting or permitting corporal punishment. Such cases are resolved through a determination of whether the punishment administered inflicted a lasting injury, or whether the punishment can be shown to have been given unjustly or with express malice.

The continuity of American public education rests squarely upon the various court decisions which relate to school law. Judicial interpretations cause meanings of the principles of governmental control over public education to change. Public school practices reflect modifications in conditions, operations, and controls. The future will demand a new type of staff, members of which will help determine the most effective means of controlling student behavior and the best means of keeping abreast of changing modes of public, professional, and legal participation in the management of the schools.

3

The Random Institution

Today's public schools were developed without planning, organization, and coordination of levels between age, maturation, ability, and student concern. Thus the schools compose a many-faceted institution. Elementary or grammer school, comprised of six to eight years (the last two may be called junior high), usually follows some form of kindergarten experience. In recent years, the preschool or early childhood training has gained great popularity as the initial step in public education. The system, composed of these three levels, has become known as the common school or elementary phase. Four years of secondary or high school education comes after two years of the seventh and eighth grade, or junior high.

Arising from local demands of separate communities, the grades grow with little reference to each other's aims, but they emerge as a culmination of parallel interests. Adult instruction, often beginning at the legal age of eighteen years, has created an additional level in the public school system. Since 1970, the expansion of specialized adult education programs has outpaced traditional high school and junior college training.

By 1850, the norm of eight years for elementary instruction had been established. Four years of secondary training was accepted across the nation by 1900. Although there was no particular basis for these divisions, most districts were organized around this "8-4" plan. The result of haphazard growth is a standard twelve years of compulsory, tax-supported education.

Both elementary and secondary school programs are informal. The divisions have always been poorly defined; there have been no true standards for entrance into any of the levels. Advancement from one grade to the next was first based on some mark of achievement in various subjects. Today, age and attendance have made such strong demands that compulsory attendance laws and age requirements very nearly supplant achievement as the requisite for advancement in the public schools.

The division process has evoked long-standing criticism from educational leaders. Beginning with the *Harvard Report* of 1892, the "8-4" pattern of school organization was bitterly attacked. Its evils and shortcomings were widely debated and, over the years, many proposals have called for broad reorganization of the entire school system.

Various revisions have been attempted. The "6-3-3" plan (six years of grammar school, three years of junior high, and three years of high school) was inaugurated in Berkeley, California, in 1909. Columbus, Ohio, and Los Angeles, California, followed in quick succession. Today schools are organized either by the "8-4" plan or some variation of the twelve year span. The majority of urban districts operate on the "6-3-3" structure.

The public may seem to show less concern with the quality of education than with the number of years needed to gain some form of certificate. The importance placed on a high school diploma or a college degree reveals society's assessment of educational achievement.

It is difficult to predict future patterns. Many indications suggest that learning opportunities will be extended from twelve to sixteen years. The accepted structure may encompass preschool, kindergarten, and six years each in both elementary and secondary instruction followed by two years of community (junior) college, trade, or technical education.

Whatever reform is attempted, none will become truly effective unless it changes the behavior of teachers and administrators who must produce a better education for students. Until new and workable concepts of organization are developed, the United States will remain a nation of schools without a system of public education.

College Added to the Ladder

College relationship to public education has been a modern development. Where once college meant private education for a few, today college-preparatory programs are a major component of the curriculum in all secondary schools. It is now the exception to find a community of any size that does not offer some form of postsecondary training. Society rejects the historic notion that further training is only for the elite. Usually two years of post high school education are open to all. The community college and adult programs are now a distinct division of public education.

Today's colleges are a far cry from the precepts of Harvard, the first college founded in the new world in 1636. Admission was restricted to Boston Latin School graduates, who were steeped in Latin, Greek, and mathematics. The university's statement of 1643 declared the function of college training to be for the education of religious ministers:

One thing we looked after was to advance Learning and perpetuate it to our Posterity . . . dreading to leave an

illiterate Ministery . . . when our present Ministers shall
lie in the Dust . . .

When scholars can read any classical work in English,
and readily make and speak Latin, and perfectly decline
nouns and verbs in the Greek tongue, they may be judged
capable of admission to Harvard . . . .

Harvard became the prototype for other colleges. Most
offered a personal education within the narrow limits of the
student's upper socioeconomic group. For two hundred years
the colleges tightly controlled much of the public schools'
curricula, dictating to the lower levels of both public and
private education.

Until it became available for the masses, the evolution of
higher education underwent no drastic revolution. The
growth of the colleges was slow until the early nineteenth
century. Then passage of the *Morrill Act* of 1862 set the direction for development of the colleges under a broad national
commitment. College expansion introduced a new function
of higher education. Advanced instruction for the many
became a public service. Tax-supported colleges were charged
with providing training in agriculture and mechanics,
governmental research, and business principles. By 1910, colleges had become a unique entity in the total educational
system. From the private undergraduate school, dominated
and administered by religious groups, the twentieth century
witnessed a multiplicity of huge institutions operated and
controlled by the several states.

Because of growing interest, postsecondary education
has brought its program to the local community. The expansion of the community college concept creates a new segment
of continued education, located in and controlled by the
public at the community level. Mass instruction now may
continue for a total of sixteen years. The community college
"falls between two schools." It is neither secondary nor
higher education, but provides elements of both. It serves
three major functions:

1. **Academic Division**—provides instruction normally required for transfer into state colleges or universities.

2. **Remedial Division**—provides students and adults with a secondary opportunity to correct deficiencies in preparation for further instruction.

3. **Vocational Division**—provides terminal instruction designed to lead to immediate employment in a trade or for personal enhancement.

Educational opportunity to enhance social life is so great that the public schools could never have met the challenge alone. Adult programs are underwritten by many established institutions and a host of governmental agencies. The actual success of adult instruction, however, rests upon the public schools because they are strategically located. They exist in every community, with facilities generally available from mid-afternoon until late at night. Schools may provide trained staff, libraries, shops, and auditoriums—all at little additional cost.

Most opposition groups, regarding education as something for children, now have been overrun by the demand for adult instruction funded by taxation. This demand belies concern over additional costs. Today only one-third of our school districts are without programs for adults.

Postsecondary education offers a challenge to all educational leaders whose professional task it is to alert the public to changing educational requirements, needs, and opportunities. It is an obligation of the schools to serve the total community which foots the educational tax bill. (It is the responsibility of educators of vision to produce the research necessary for workable reorganization that will meet the demands of adult programs.) Radical changes in school operation and management at every level should be on drawing boards now.

Who's in Charge

Early in our country's history, the local district was considered to be the largest unit practicable and effective for school operation. This belief was based upon the fact that transportation was slow and communication between isolated communities was lacking. The local school district and its school board became an arm separate from the body of its town—it controlled local education.

The original districts were established to operate elementary schools. When secondary schools became legal, tuition-free, tax-supported institutions, they were first administered by elementary school districts. Sometimes, two or more combined to form Joint, Consolidated, or Union districts. The local unit of school control began to vary in size, from the one room school system to a city district requiring teachers for thousands of pupils.

In an effort to provide better education, alternatives to the local school district have been adopted from time to time. But in no area have the pattern and goals of districts been identical. In the north and west, a district was usually consolidated around a central high school and its several feeder elementary schools. In other areas, district boundaries were established to be coterminous with the city or county. As a result, several types of administrative patterns may now be found throughout the United States.

1.   **Rural District**—usually too small to support a wide program of education.

2.   **Union or Joint District**—formed by joining two or more rural areas to support a program of secondary education.

3. **Town or Township District**—formed inside arbitrary boundaries within the total area.

4. **Consolidated District**—comprised of several township districts to provide a broader tax base for education support.

5. **Community District**—formed wherever people in an area can identify with common needs and organize around some focal issue.

6. **City or Independent District**—formed when a city becomes separate and distinct from the township or county government.

7. **County District**—the largest administrative unit providing central authority for all schools in the county.

Expansion of the district has become a primary reason for the creation of administrative units large enough to finance an adequate program of instruction. The *Lancasterian System* (originated in Lancaster, Pennsylvania), which permitted one school teacher to teach many pupils at a very small cost per child, provided an enormous stimulus to public education. In 1843, the cost of education in New York City was less than two dollars per child per year. Reduction in the cost of public education became the major criterion for widespread acceptance of tax-supported schools.

Changing conditions of the twentieth century have made the local district system appear obsolete. It is argued that smaller districts have been incorporated into larger administrative units within the concept of local control because responsibility is in the hands of a board of education elected by the voters in each component area.

People display a great tenacity whenever any shifts in control from the locality to a larger unit is considered. Any district reorganization becomes a political issue. State legislatures, which must approve reorganization, are often dominated by rural representatives. Accordingly, lawmakers have been slow to increase the size of the school districts.

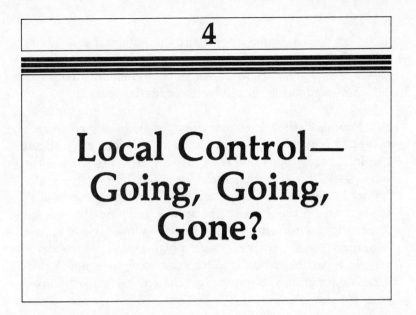

4

Local Control— Going, Going, Gone?

The United States has been called a nation of small school systems financed by inadequate tax bases. Small districts retard the creation of effective administrative units for more comprehensive programs. But perhaps the greatest weakness of the small district system is its inability to establish proper coordination of the educational program from kindergarten through the adult levels of instruction.

Whatever the reason, the small school district is on the way out. The direction of educational control swings away from the community, first to the county, then to the state, and, finally, to the national government.

There are three major criteria by which to judge the size and character of school districts:

1. **Physical resources.** Resources should be large enough to support an adequate educational program from kindergarden through adult levels.

2. **Common traditions.** District populations should represent people with common aims.

3. **Unity.** District voters should identify with their community and have a commitment to it.

Political issues determine why people in any given area accept or reject district reorganization, and they are difficult to pinpoint. Perhaps one reason is the attitudes toward the old system. An area unaffected by population shifts usually favors traditional school patterns. Wherever strong feelings support an existing tax rate, programs, or some professional leader, the sentiments favor the *status quo.* Newly built suburban centers, however, with a high mobility of residents who lack particular bonds to tradition, seek to establish progressive programs. Support for change leads to modified roles for the schools.

The reduction in the total number of school districts in the United States, from nearly 100,000 in 1946 to less than 15,000 in 1974, does not guarantee better schools or more efficient management. Unification of poor districts can only produce larger and still more inefficient systems.

Most reorganization has followed the lead taken in mushrooming areas during the last three decades. Because growth has peaked, the stage is now set for an era of declining enrollment. This decline raises problems of decentralization. A further reorganization to resolve new issues must be accomplished. Areas overbuilt with schools must come forward with valid plans for different uses of existing facilities, such as expansion of adult programs. Today's administrative task is to provide a new public relationship, to create community confidence for the support of the total school program.

School district reorganization means more than changes in administrative management. Professional educators must understand that a desire to improve the teaching program may not always be congruent with factors supporting change. Continuation of the battle between educators and politicians will become even more acute, for there is no doubt that the educational system is intimately associated with politics. The two institutions could not survive separation. Because an underlying principle of any government is to ensure its own continuity, an ever growing relationship between education and national politics is inevitable. The nature and extent of that relationship is crucial.

Limits of the School Board

The responsibility for school operation is vested in boards of education. Acting for the will of the voters and utilizing broad powers granted by legislatures, the school board has a function that is unique to American education. Other nations administer their schools by provincial or municipal governments under a federal minister of education. Local citizens participate only in necessary advisory capacities.

The American concept of an elected school board is an outgrowth of the colonial town council. An interim step provided school committees, formed to select and evaluate teachers. Over the years, such lay control evolved into local boards of education to operate schools.

A board in the larger districts usually delegates the responsibility for running the schools to a professional administrative staff. The board retains only the policy-making function. In theory, the staff may carry out only those actions that have been determined by adopted policy.

A district board of education, often comprised of community leaders, is normally elected on a nonpartisan basis. It is controlled in at least two ways. It may exercise only the limited authority granted to it by the state, and its members may serve only a fixed term of office. They must be re-elected by the people if they wish to continue their services.

Perhaps the greatest responsibility of any local board is the function it serves as a communications exchange between public and professional staff. One reason for communications failure is because there are no funds allocated for an effective staff through which either the schools' superintendent or the board may operate. This failure has often brought about the downfall of boards, superintendents, or both. A change of administration and defeat of incumbent board members are basic ingredients of our system of checks and balances.

In practice, a school board is a decision-making group. Seldom does a board meet to deliberate an agenda without decisions on which to vote. Open discussion culminates in a vote, and majority vote enables the adoption of policy. This is the political process of bargain and compromise to define and resolve community issues.

Personal and public goals may come into direct conflict. A board may desire to maintain a low tax rate while facing the need for additional facilities and staff. Any decision brings action and reaction from community factions, and the political process related to the next board election begins. Board members are responsible and accountable for their action.

Many people wish the functions of a board of education could be eradicated by law, believing that its service is eroded beyond repair, and that its days are numbered. The most pronounced opposition to board authority has come from union-type teacher associations.

The function of school boards has been under scrutiny by political scientists, professional administrators, and state lawmakers. Charges are made that public education has suffered because of unilateral decisions made by boards, often in the name of political response to some vested interest within the community. Charges have also been made that boards, comprised of leading businessmen and women, have become a democratic liability. The claim is made that members represent small-minded, autocratic leaders whose main effort is to keep taxes under tight control. Many board opponents would remove the purse strings from local control and place financial responsibility for education in the hands of the state and national governments. School boards would be reduced to arbitrating trivia.

If, in the opinion of some, boards have already committed suicide, the death of local control of the schools will surely mark a turning point in the long history of public education. Education would be controlled, as it is practiced in most nations of the world, by state and national government. Such a takeover was rejected first by the colonial settlers. Their position has been upheld for over 300 years of development.

5

The Tax Dollar

Since the public education is a legal function of state government, the legislature establishes general requirements, operational constraints, and basic financial support. Political control of school operations at the local level is a basic concept in our system. School financing, from the beginning, has posed a difficult problem, and the future will be no exception. Any increase in school taxes will always create public controversy. Educational costs will remain a problem since school taxes depend upon the people's willingness to support programs. The degree of financial support imposes an enormous control over programs.

Few taxpayers enjoy paying taxes for schools. They seek a bargain; they look for ways to get the most for their tax dollar. One of the most important tasks of school administrators is to show clearly the relationship between budgeted items and the quality and quantity of instruction. In most areas across the nation, for good or ill, professional educators have failed to carry out this function. Many seem to ignore the fact that education is controlled by the tax support received.

The greatest single control over public schools is the economic attitude of the time. Public education has always been directly influenced by economic conditions. Conversely, the creativity and productivity of educated people affect the economy. They play a major role in shaping economic conditions. By constantly upgrading qualifications for workers and by concentrating plants in urban areas, business and industry have placed increasing demands upon the schools. Yet school values seem remote to a working public which has to be willing to underwrite the costs of expanding education. Any effort on the part of schools to meet new demands increases the cost of education. Even though an expanding economy enlarges the tax base upon which schools depend, schools have to struggle to keep pace.

Public education has always had to be responsive to economic change. During the latter half of the eighteenth century, most colonial schools began to include courses to meet the time's needs. Curricula listings indicated instruction in bookkeeping, surveying, and navigation. When the "academy," our public high school, was born, other vocational courses were added which crowded out much of classical education.

The post-Civil War era brought a need for engineers and mechanics. Passage of the *Morrill Act* of 1862 enabled the establishment of land-grant and state colleges by allowing the federal government to provide the land on the condition that such institutions offer courses in agriculture and the mechanical arts. Immediate pressure was then applied on elementary and secondary schools to revise curriculum.

The twentieth century has seen a proliferation of courses in the secondary schools. Even though the college preparatory program still remains the major offering, the *Smith-Hughes Act* of 1917 created federal funds for establishing vocational curricula.

The public schools responded to the great depression of the thirties by inaugurating programs to prepare youth for life. This concept of general education designed to meet social, political, and economic challenges was the accepted theory following World War II. The 1960s brought a wave of industrial courses to meet an era of automation. In the 1970s, a three-pronged response was made to prevailing economic conditions:

1. Increased attention to the science and mathematics courses

2. Expansion of the technical, trade, and leisure time education

3. Return to an emphasis on the basic skills

Taxation of Property

The oldest, most common form of school financing comes from a direct property tax. Such a tax is normally levied by the local board of education, regardless of the size of the district, in an amount below a maximum determined by the state legislature. The amount of property tax available for school revenues is based upon the assessed valuation of property affected. When the assessed valuation is equated to some unit of public education, such as the cost per attending child, an index showing the comparative wealth of districts may be established. Results of every study indicate a wide discrepancy between a district's purported ability to finance the public schools and its actual ability. There may have been a time when property values provided a fair indication of possible income. But shifts of population from rural to urban areas, changes from agrarian to industrial society, and property mortgages have made this obsolete.

The major evils of the property tax system have been due to wide variations in assessing values, the exemption of people who own no property, and the fact that the assessed valuation does not reflect the true ability of an area to finance its public schools. Financial inequity prohibits equal educational opportunities from becoming a reality.

The ability of school districts to raise money varies tremendously. There is also a wide variation in the ability of the several states to support their respective educational programs. The many assessment practices differ considerably, and the assessed values per pupil prove of little consequence when comparing state and school finances. One state practice provides an unusual example.

> A resident of a northern State owns a vacation home, located in Florida, which is currently assesed at $16,000. The annual property tax bill is about $315, of which a majority goes for direct school support. As an absentee owner, with no children enrolled in Florida schools, his tax bill may be compared to that of a neighbor who resides directly across the steet. Living in a home assessed at the identical value, the neighbor sends three children to the local schools, but pays a total property tax bill of just $28, of which a majority also goes for educational support. The difference stems from a "Homestead Exemption" for bona fide Florida residents.

Several schemes have been used to apportion state school funds. None has proved fully successful. Educators have had to look to new means and additional sources for revenues and they are quick to see a long history of federal aid. To some, such federal expenditures provide a logical solution.

Federal aid to the states for school expenditures has been nearly all categorical in nature. Much of it has been administered through colleges and universities with the apparent intent to upgrade programs and personnel training. The overall amount of federal expenditure forms only a tiny portion of the total cost of public education.

State aid programs, in most cases, do not correct the unequal ability of local districts to finance their programs.

Nor do federal grants help poor districts raise sufficient revenues. The problem remains acute.

Fears over potential loss of local control have created an outcry against federal school financing. Perhaps such concern dates back to the ancient Hebrew kingdom under David. That nation was divided and subdivided into districts for local affairs. But these districts were kept under the political jurisdiction of a type of national court system, and the court's judges were appointed by the king. In this way, all local control vested in the old tribes was stamped out. David had built a central government based on tightfisted authority to overcome local rule.

Thirty years later, Solomon replaced the tribal divisions with taxing regions that cut across the old tribal lines of power. The political entity of local regions became subservient to the national government; the local tax base came under centralized control.

Centuries later, the same principles were incorporated in the American Constitution. The state powers were made lesser than national authority, but many controls were reserved to the people of the respective states. The end of state and local power will come when both are forced to depend upon the central government for finances.

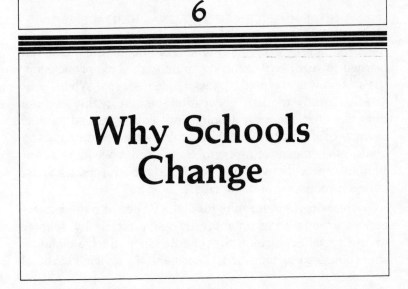

6

Why Schools Change

A philosophy of education in our country rests not on a solid foundation of orderly historical development, but on a base both tenuous and intangible. Purposes of the schools have emerged through fragmented additions to curricula and, in the process, have created surprising inconsistencies. The air has never been cleared of important questions. What is public education, and what are its aims? How are the schools organized to accomplish education's aims? What part do the taxpayers play in determining the role of the schools? How are teachers and administrators trained, selected, and evaluated? By what means is the system measured? In what direction is public education moving?

Answers to these questions constitute an outline of public goals, a set of objectives, and a determination of structure. But many a school program is geared to its own peculiar aims and goals. Most people perceive the system from their own point of view.

As long as the basic goals centered on the mastery of the three R's (Reading, Writing, and Arithmetic), educators were provided with a known yardstick for evaluation that would meet the approval of the public. As long as most children learned to read, write, and compute with some proficiency, the system was accepted by the people it served. When "progressive" and "modern" education became reality, school objectives became more vague. Both educators and parents became confused because they could not agree on common goals, nor a means of assessing them. Today we have a continuous conflict between the public, administrators, teachers, college professors, and students.

Breakdowns in meaningful dialogue between these interrelated groups bring on more intensive efforts by splinter groups to gain control of the school system. Such a dictatorship could lead to educational chaos and the system's eventual collapse.

Aims Forever Argued

People know that differences of opinion exist about the nature of educational purposes, methods of instruction, and means to evaluate achievement. Few realize that this controversy is as old as civilization. Historically, the aims of education have always been divided into conservative and progressive elements.

The ancient Chinese conducted schools to instruct youth for the preservation of the state order. Athenian instruction was aimed at the development of well-rounded character, a balance between the academic, moral, and physical needs. Basic skills were included to improve the individual's usefulness to his society. The early Romans introduced education for the practical values of acceptable citizenship. Judeo-Christian purposes centered on preparation for an afterlife, while the Renaissance brought a revival of liberal instruction for this world's cultural pleasures.

Following the Protestant Revolution, the aims of education were described as classical; instruction was concerned only with nonmaterialistic goals. The American colonies, searching for religious and political freedom, offered instruction aimed at strengthening liberty and democracy. During the early decades of the twentieth century, educational goals were expressed by the progressive aims: "life adjustment" for the good of the individual.

The role of the schools, in relation to other social agencies helping youth to understand its environment, remains a subject of national debate. The *White House Conference Report* of 1955 stated most current goals of public education from the point of view of a "liberal" philosophy. Today, most school objectives encompass those listed in the *Education Policies Commission Report* of 1963. Current goals revolve around an identified central purpose of education: *freedom of the mind through instruction in the rational powers.*

Modern purposes of education give a complex and comprehensive character to the schools. Public instruction is expected to meet the enormous challenge of providing meaningful education to all youth. As a result of universal, compulsory education, the great debate over education's goals fills the air in every community.

At the midpoint of the 1970s, critics demanded reduced expenditures through returning curricula to basic disciplines. Efforts to gain control of the schools to force a return to fundamentals grows ever stronger as the economic base grows weaker. The hope for the system rests on the establishment now of a nationally revised, reliable form of public evaluation of school, teacher, and pupil achievement.

The Puritan concept of education created a restrictive system of schools, open mostly to those in the upper social strata. The core of the curriculum rested on the academics, to prepare youths for college. When the number of secondary schools grew to open new opportunities for the poor, the program remained college-prep in nature. Secondary schools developed into institutions in which scholarship grants put needy but deserving students on the rolls. For over 300 years, colleges have controlled the curricula of all levels of public education.

Dating from the Constitutional Convention of 1787, the republic was awash in waves of educational reform. National leaders, building a democratic government that could exist only as long as the individual citizen was able to understand political issues, nurtured the seed of curriculum expansion. Nineteenth century schools broke abruptly from their traditional three R's to set the stage for a unique system of universal instruction.

The European school system included the *gymnasium, lyceum,* and the college for those pupils between the ages of ten and twenty whose parents could afford the tuition. From this practice of education for the elite, American schools developed into a free system of public instruction. Following eight years of elementary training in the fundamental skills of reading, writing, and arithmetic, all youth could expect education to continue through the community college level. While the European process remained socially aloof, the American system became a bold instrument to support the democratic experience.

A national *Committee of Ten,* in an extensive report issued in 1896, proclaimed that college preparatory education could be considered the most appropriate form of instruction for life itself. The result forced educators to accept an elementary curriculum designed to prepare all youth for high school. American youth would receive academic instruction as the basic preparation for college and for life. Commercial and vocational education were considered as elective training. The schools of the modern era were molded into a kind of people's schools system, where the needs of the largest number could be served at the lowest cost.

Public instruction's academic base was modified by the philosophy of John Dewey and others who were able to fuse the concept of social training to the overall curriculum. In the first fifty years of the twentieth century, educational reform was triumphant, and anyone who sought to retain only the three R's was suspect. The age of experimentation reigned supreme in the public schools until by the early 1940s, "progressive education" had become the master of most professional educators.

Not everyone embraced the new order. A few still wished to return to the avatar of the three R's. Others sought to establish a curriculum based on science and intelligence, making the schools an instrumental base on which a new society could be built. The argument ran that all school subjects must enable youth to make selective judgments from a host of alternatives ever present in the affluent society. In political terms, those against the new order were the conservative; those for it were given the progressive label.

Both groups have lost their sense of direction. They do constant battle, each accusing the other of capturing control of public instruction. While the debate between traditionalist and progressive rages, a generation of boys and girls remains free to select a strange blend of academic and "social adjustment" courses. To the layman, the school system appears disorganized, and without reliable leadership. Everyone feels compromised. But the real loser is youth. The educator of vision must question the major purposes of public education for the next generation.

In the past twenty-five years, those demanding reforms to replace progressive instruction base arguments on cost, methods, curriculum, and training—all in relationship to the public's evaluation. People are now asking questions, criticizing, and condemning progressive education. Many wonder when public instruction should actually begin. Others observe that training may occur outside the school term, daytime hours, and school buildings. Students currently ask why schools cannot provide preparation for a career as well as that necessary for college entrance. Educators suggest that achievement at any particular level should permit a student to take the next step in a total life process of learning.

Adapt or Die

The aims of schools may be described as broad expressions of community demands, subject to constant revision. The definition of good citizenship might not be acceptable in all communities alike, and the social attributes of good citizenship may differ from one generation to another. Education expresses the needs of society at some particular point in time only, and no school system will be supported long without community approval and support.

The major learning objectives of public education can be grouped under two separate goals. First, goals that the schools can define, teach, and measure. The basic three R's fall into this group. Second, goals that are difficult to define and impractical to evaluate, such as the incidental instruction of good citizenship.

Earliest school aims were directly related to student mastery of the three R's. Evaluation of school and teacher competence, based on these known objectives, was simple, limited, and easily demonstrated to parents. Achievement could be measured in terms readily accepted by the public. As community pressure added courses to the curriculum, the school and the educator were caught in a crossfire. School aims ran ahead of any objective ways to determine instructional success. This dilemma still faces the modern educator as he attempts to equate current social demands for more schooling with rational standards of achievement.

Economic considerations exert heavy pressures on the instructional process. Most aims of public education have been established to satisfy some particular pressure from the community. The majority have come because of public demand to meet a crisis caused by economic downturn. The creativity and productivity of educated people have always had a hand in shaping the economy which, in turn, affects the tax structure supporting schools. Periodic revisions in goals are the direct result of economic fluctuations. The industrial search for new products goes hand in hand with business growth. Both depend upon the educational system. Even the growth of labor unions has determined much of the teaching content and methods of the public schools. Indeed, curricular revision is often the result of demand exerted on schools by citizen groups who may represent no real broad segment of the public. In knee jerk fashion, the system responds, and expanded instruction results—at the expense of the fundamental tasks of the schools.

The public must understand, however, that not all objectives expected of the schools are subject to evaluation. Once this fact can be communicated, time, effort, and money can be redirected to create better instruction. The underlying truth of educational evaluation is that an objective measurement of school achievement is applicable only to the fundamental processes. Reading, writing, arithmetic, and certain kinds of specialized courses can be evaluated, and in terms that reflect specific degrees of achievement by teacher and student.

The continuity of a democratic, free nation under its cherished principles of representative government is the only criterion by which education can be considered effective. Unfortunately, this measurement of success can be made only after the fact and by succeeding generations. Understanding the governmental process and good citizenship cannot be evaluated by testing factual knowledge memorized through rote learning.

Systems are labeled "good" or "bad" by a misinformed public's subjective measurement. They are held accountable for the education of the children, and the success or failure of instruction—processes for which they are not totally responsible.

Two concepts are basic to an understanding of the school's responsibility:

1.   The school system is only one among many institutions from which the child learns, and what he

learns from his total environment may support or conflict with school instruction.

2. Learning occurs concurrently in multi-settings during the school age years, which may be extended throughout one's entire life.

One particular state curriculum and course of study guide reflects the purposes of public schools. Parts of this state Code, enacted during the mid-1940s and still binding on the schools of that state, are cited to indicate the extent that written curricular mandates go beyond basic and traditional tasks of the schools.

Public education is an obligation of society in our own democracy. The schools are responsible for providing instructional opportunities for group growth and development of all citizens from kindergarten through adulthood.

The instructional objectives of public education encompass the total goals of democracy. But the schools, family, church, community, and other social institutions share the major responsibilities of well adjusted citizens.

1. School boards shall provide for the health, well-being, and training of all pupils . . . as part of the course of study regularly taught in the schools of this state.

2. The nature of alcohol and other narcotic drugs and their effects on the human system shall be taught throughout the several grades in the school systems in this state.

3. Every teacher in every grade and subject shall teach pupils honesty, kindness, justice, and moral courage . . . One-half hour each week shall be devoted to teaching humane treatment of animals.

4. American patriotism and principles of representative government, as enunciated in the Declaration of Independence, the Constitution, and the state constitution, and the proper use and display of the American flag shall be taught in all public schools . . . Instruction shall be

given in the method of voting by means of the Australian ballot.

5. No pupil shall be graduated from any public high school in this state unless he has received instruction in the history of the United States and gives satisfactory evidence of having a comprehensive understanding thereof.

At public demand, schools revise method, type, and extent of learning activities, but when the day can accommodate no more, subjects are dropped, combined, or cut in content; the basic three R's are pushed aside. Perhaps it is time to reverse the process. Is there some instruction for which the home, church, or employer might better take on responsibility anew?

Administrator—Agent of Change

The administrative structure of public schools reflects social customs, political institutions, and business practices of the nation, states and local communities. Its development and established operation and purpose reflect the expectations of the public. But the struggle to keep pace with changing conditions to maintain this harmony depends upon the leadership provided by professional educators.

As society advances, the educational institution becomes more and more complex. In the modern political structure, people have delegated decision-making rights to those who are declared professional experts. Though delegated, people retain those rights. They simply depend upon their elected representatives to set policy for educators to administer. All groups today may—and do—express their desires regarding educational directions to those they elect to legislate.

That the public, its elected representatives, and the educators understand their respective roles is vital. Each must support the other to provide the best possible educational programs. This exchange of confidence rests squarely on the school administrator's effective leadership.

The role of superintendent as the leader for educational change is unique. Several basic duties cover diverse assignments, each designed to please a multitude of community groups. He is an executive, yet he carries out the duties of a policy adviser, an educational authority, and a civic leader. Perhaps the greatest task of the urban district superintendent is to act as buffer between public, staff members, and board of education.

The chief administrative officer is accountable for formulating and proposing educational policies for the development of curricular programs. When he submits his recommendations to the school board, he becomes legal counselor to the elected governing body. In normal practice, every board relies on its superintendent to produce workable policies pointing out the correct direction.

Theoretically, the superintendent introduces only those proposals for change which he will support. Unless he urges adoption of recommendations, they have little chance for acceptance by the board. Ordinarily, neither the public nor the elected board introduces major modifications or programs to the system. In certain cases, teacher groups and citizen committees may bypass normal channels of communication by submitting proposals for change directly to the board. Such suggestions might also be released to the news media in an effort to apply pressure. Until the board receives an administrative analysis, however, adoption is rarely approved. The most significant changes in public education are engineered by and through the superintendent.

After approval of a proposed policy by the board, the superintendent, in his administrative function, implements necessary action. At this point, his job becomes even more delicate. He must satisfy the board, staff members, and the community at large. Boldness, patience, and effective action are necessary, and all may be crucial to far more than just a single policy. The superintendent may be forced to modify his organizational structure. He must find the money to operate in a pre-existing budget. He must identify and locate the right staff and facilities needed. Perhaps the personnel functions are most critical. The effectiveness of any program depends upon staff competence.

As the chief agent for educational improvement, the superintendent is subject to countless pressures. In order to direct and coordinate successfully the functions of the school district, the board, administration, staff, parents, students, and public must remain supportive. He will meet conflicting demands of divergent groups and organizations. The various roles he must play are likely to require an array of staff talent. The urban district superintendent cannot function without special assistants, each carefully selected and trained to provide unique contributions. The major aim of the administrative team is toward educational change for improvement. Any other purpose only shortchanges the instructional offerings for pupils of each succeeding generation.

Whenever a decision for educational change is made and administered, the role of the system is redirected. Revised strategies emerge out of changed attitudes, either in support of or in opposition to the new goals. In our form of democracy, a change in any one social institution often creates resistance by other agencies.

Because the school system faces frequent demands for change, it feels the greatest pressures from the widest segments of the community. Professional educators are easily trapped and they often must speedily redefine priorities and objectives. Superintendents, school boards, and teachers often turn away from basic issues to compromise, to save the main mission as they see it—the maintenance of the system—jettisoning educational improvement.

Current administrative practice depends upon curricular planning with citizen participation. This can be inefficient, ineffective, and deceitful. It can undermine and disrupt all forms of productive school-community relations. In one sense, citizen participation in curricular projects is undemocratic, because of prejudiced appointments—like calls to like. Neither educators, nor school boards, nor community members on such committees face the real issues of what the school should do, why it should do it, how it may best be done at what cost, and how the results can be measured.

Even the purpose for seeking community participation in school planning is often replete with double meaning. When boards of education and superintendents resort to citizen involvement, they are often dodging their own responsibilities. If the public has a hand in formulating goals, curriculum, and methods, then the community must be satisfied. Accountability for school failures can be shifted to the public.

Whenever a particular attack on the school erupts, it is common practice for the superintendent to counter emotion by calling for a citizens' committee to study the issues and make recommendations. Charging a lay group of unsophisticated and diverse community leaders to come forth with recommendations at best places false confidence in a political group process, and, at worst, is a hypocritical act. Each member, no matter how selected or appointed, will represent a pressure segment of the community. Some seek to have the superintendent dismissed. Others propose to alter methods or curriculum. A few hope to replace the current board. Some come to the committee with a particular viewpoint and an intolerance for any other.

Future instructional improvements must be dependent upon a workable system to create good community relations. Any board of education dedicated to effective schools will achieve that goal only when school-community relations foster the necessary support. The responsibility for action rests with the board; implementation falls upon the superintendent; but the results of action are in the hands of the entire staff. None will survive unless good will is earned by an open exchange of information operating through workable channels under the direction of a new breed of public educator.

7

A Tour of the Battlegrounds

The American public schools are in serious trouble. Students, parents, educators, and lawmakers hurl general indictments at the public school system. Discontent is voiced by every element of society. After fifty years of experimental and innovative patterns, progressive practices are failing.

Too many classrooms use boring and inefficient materials, procedures, and techniques. The schools are out of step with modern needs, off base from current economic demand, and years behind social changes. Adults, educators, and millions of students are turned off.

Criticism of the schools is considered a profitable pastime. Journalists, educators, and parents write and speak about visible ills; their books, periodicals, editorials, and speeches reflect a uniformity of attack upon experimental practices. Current criticism, unlike that of the past, enjoys a growing audience.

Communities once proud of their schools have changed attitudes. A curriculum that includes anything more than instruction in the basic skills is once again questioned. Citizens have tried to force inclusion of tougher courses requiring higher achievement standards. Some communities have shown a desire to understand the methods of measurement. They will make all-out efforts to control such methods and bring them to community standards.

We hear ever increasing wails against costly programs of innovation. Taxpayers expect proper accomplishment. Thoughtful educators are listening; they know these signals well. The signals are society's increasing pressure for proven educational results based on an acceptable means of public evaluation.

Two Basic Philosophies

Each of the major purposes of education rests on a philosophical base. They may be defined two ways. *One:* "education" may refer to every experience that effects a change in an individual. This training never ceases. Each experience throughout one's life may be educational. *Two:* "education," in a more restrictive sense, may be considered as the process of creating specific experiences to provide acceptable values and skills.

Educators, lawmakers, and citizens often do not agree on these definitions. No generally accepted theory defines values or skills, nor is opinion concerted on selection of appropriate goals—all of which leads to disagreement over operation, control, and finances.

Many attempts have been made to improve the quality of public instruction. Each is hailed as a concrete action to upgrade practices. Efforts are made to expand or combine several disciplinary subjects into revitalized courses. Curriculum studies and reports are professional contributions to the search for higher quality. But present citizen concern centers almost exclusively on a return to the fundamental skills as the major purpose of the school system.

The earliest attempts to modify the "lockstep" method of instruction—the student is lectured by the instructor and recites the lecture back—became plans to individualize learning experiences. The lecture-recitation practice was abolished in Pueblo, Colorado, as early as 1888. Students were encouraged to advance at their individual speed. This revolutionary program was doomed. Neither staff nor public would accept the change. Without community support, the effort failed.

Twenty-five years later, a systematized program of individualized instruction was developed for the training school at San Francisco State College. The staff prepared "self-directed" study materials for students. Group assignments and all lecture-recitations were eliminated. Each student worked out the written materials at his individual rate. The teacher performed twin duties, to direct and evalute. When a particular assignment was completed, the student was tested and handed a new task. Both the *Dalton* (Massachusetts) and *Winnetka* (Illinois) Plans were adaptations of this individualized "learning packet" concept.

These pioneer developments stimulated the search to find a system to break the old instructional procedures. Modern programs of individualized learning stem from this exploration. But the underlying philosophy of instruction for the masses remained, and remains, strong. That at least one goal of the school should be to encompass personal development through individualized instruction is agreed. The emphasis on this purpose appears healthy. No one disputes the aim to help students develop individual abilities. The controversy arises over purposes, practices, costs, and evaluation procedures.

Some believe that preoccupation with individualized instruction may be self-defeating. Schools have undertaken countless programs to raise academic achievement by speeding up student progress through individualized instruction. Important as this may be, personal attention is only one part of the educational function. In the modern era, public schools cannot restrict their objectives solely to the development of students as individuals. Practical education must harmonize the goals of individual instruction with citizenship training if the school system is to achieve its purpose. That purpose is to train people to share the rights and responsibilities of citizenship.

Local, State, Federal Concerns

Public education is a constitutional function reserved to the state by virtue of the American heritage of separation of powers, but is of vital concern to the national government. The organization and operation of the schools have been delegated by the state to the local community under some form of district administrative process. Under various degrees of local control, the mechanics of school organization are an outgrowth of persistent distrust of centralized authority over educational endeavor.

The wariness of citizens toward concentration of governmental power has affected the typical management pattern of public education. The traditional desire for layer-type control of any governmental function is best shown by the concerns for the school system. While there is a national interest in the concept of universal education, the process remains under state control. Yet the local community operates the schools, within legal limits, to reflect the wishes of local citizens. The traditional school district operating under an elected board has come to symbolize local control of public education.

Professional students of public education consider the local district concept to be a unique mechanism. Local responsibility for the schools has evolved into a home-neighborhood-community-school partnership that has no counterpart in any other nation. It is a partnership replete with inherent weaknesses.

Regardless of the number of state attempts to provide equalization of financial support, broad variations in the type, extent, and quality of instruction remain. Since a major portion of school funds is derived from the local property tax, poor communities tend to operate poorly financed systems. The great differences in educational opportunities create critical problems extending across the entire nation. When people move from the community where they attended school, the matter of unequal education is removed from the state to become a national concern. Reform movements stemming from a nationalizing influence on school operation may well engulf local communities, and both state and federal participation in all areas of the school programs expand.

In no way does this outlook imply that the local-state-federal partnership in local education need be abolished. Proper reform could actually strengthen such relationships.

Recent reorganizational practices have reduced the number and inceased the size of school districts. The result has eroded neighborhood patterns of school operations. New policies, revised divisions of grade levels, and greater emphasis on location, facilities, and structures have created a situation in which the schools are no longer a community unifying force. Indeed, many a community voice now calls for decentralization, seeking a breakup of districts into smaller entities.

Those who are ever fearful of any movement toward smaller organizational units are turning to the idea of the county as the direct manager of the public schools. They favor an enlarged school-community area. Such advocates of expansion certainly place increased emphasis on consolidation of all governmental agencies to effect a reduction of taxes. If carried to its logical conclusion, the school system would be controlled and operated by the county supervisors. Public control of the schools would be removed even further from local community citizens.

No fixed norms exist for the determination of community or neighborhood size, population, or wealth. But the traditional pattern of school organization needs revision. Grassroots democracy has several advantages, but to some, the local school district system is outmoded and unworkable. The by-now-common method of reorganization, by which small districts are combined or absorbed into larger units, is itself becoming impractical. A revolutionary structure for school administration is necessary, possible, and feasible.

Who's A Professional?

Historically, classroom teachers have been accepted as the focal point of the entire instructional process. They are characterized by many a stereotype, the original, perhaps, being Washington Irving's Ichabod Crane. Even the old Hoosier schoolmaster has his place as an example of the typical teacher. As late as the 1940s, the teacher was accepted as the only adult in the classroom—a kind of Mr. Chips, educator and friend to all, teaching the world's heritage, a mentor of pupils and a molder of men.

Buildings, subjects, equipment, administrators, and pupils took second place. Specialized support and clerical personnel were mere factotums. Millions of people believed that master teachers alone created good schools.

Such a fixed idea has been shattered. The responsibilities of education require more divisions and classifications of teachers; their role has been expanded. Teachers are called supervisors, coordinators, directors, principals, and superintendents. Differentiation of functions has developed particular needs for specialized tasks. In one sense, all are teachers, but not all are called instructors.

American educator, Mark Hopkins, once defined a school as a log with a teacher on one end and a student on the other. He was describing the two essential features of a school. But today, greater emphasis is placed on books, equipment, buildings, services, and support personnel. Today, most people believe that a school is far more than just teacher and pupil. Whatever their function, staff members of modern school systems are called educators.

Education constitutes much more than training in a school. It is a process of learning to do and to think, based on a mastery of the fundamental skills. Success of the process, as demanded by public support, must be measured in terms of pupil achievement. No other evaluation is valid. The teacher is only part of the total force constituting the learning environment.

In the early years of American educational history, teachers were selected haphazardly. The criterion was the ability to maintain discipline. Little else was expected, and nothing else was asked. The development of a public school system brought demands for higher standards in teacher preparation. Higher levels of education were required.

The first teacher training school was established in 1823 at Concord, Vermont. Instruction was at the level of the academy (a general high school level), but courses in methods and schoolkeeping were included as part of the curriculum. New York established the first county teacher training schools in 1827. Soon most elementary teachers were graduates of the academy or teacher training schools. High school teachers were expected to have completed some college instruction.

The first state-supported normal school for teacher training was established in Lexington, Massachusetts, in 1840, under the direction of Horace Mann. The concept spread into other areas. At the turn of the twentieth century, more than two hundred teacher training institutions were in operation. The normal school developed as an extension of the grade school and high school to reach equivalent status of a college. As standards were raised and curricula expanded, the normal school became the forerunner of state teachers colleges. By the 1950s, state teachers colleges had evolved into multi-purpose state universities. Any difference between teacher training and other branches of higher education disappeared during the 1960s.

Reform Cannot Wait

Educators, like the schools and communities in which they work, are heterogeneous. There are all kinds, representing all shades of competencies. No one will deny their influence over the minds of youth. Nor will anyone belittle their social significance. The fact is that all citizens who go to school receive their training from some educator. Since public education is a state function, and is based on compulsory attendance laws, educators perform a vital service to the individual, the community, the state, and the nation. The educator affects every segment in our society.

Widespread disagreement exists over the curricula of teacher training institutions. Programs for preparation vary widely from state to state and from college to college. Common understanding of content, theory, and requirements for entrance into the profession are missing. Training programs' lack of consistency results in demands for an overall upgrading of teacher certification. Today's charges of teacher training's low quality represent an attack on the entire educational system. Many people claim that incompetent educators man the public schools because of liberalized training programs. The attack centers on the dispute over what the teacher knows and how she or he is able to teach it. Traditional demand is to increase academic preparation, while others seek expansion of teaching methods. The philosophical battle rages over whether *what* to teach is more important than *how* to teach—and vice versa.

Critics of teacher training condemn the so-called methods courses. When specific educators are charged with incompetency, the attack is on methods. When a parent says, "You don't know how to teach," there is little training in the *how*. Ironically, people seem to believe that a professional group can survive without training that includes the basis for professional practice. Lack of knowledge makes methods worthless; practice of methods is meaningless without knowledge.

Educators know methods cannot be considered in opposition to content. The two components of educational training cannot be isolated one from the other. No medical doctor is licensed because he passes an examination on *what* he is taught; he must be able to practice the *how* of his learning, too. The educator, also, must understand both content and method. The profession at large, however, has failed to communicate this interrelationship to the public. Continuing attacks on teacher training now center on certain base motives of college and educator.

Graduate courses in "Strategies for Change," in which educators learn how to carry out modification of the instructional process, may have meaning for the professional educator. To the public, such courses are suspect. Courses in methods and strategies, educators claim, develop hard skills in diagnosis, communications, resources, the organization of parental support, the creation of favorable public relations, and taking action. The colleges predict such training will bring out greater competency in working with students and parents.

The public remains unconvinced. It sees no improvement in the content that youth is expected to be taught. Parents are wary over changes discussed by educators. They become frightened because they see no way to demand objective performance evaluation of staff and students. Distrust of the emerging educator, intent on school change, has reached the point of condemnation of the entire system. Today's opinion is that it is time to reform the mission of public education. Many believe that changes must take place first in the training programs of the educators.

Some critics would even be satisfied with gradual change over another generation. Their attitude begs the question.

Neither the public nor the lawmaker will wait while pupil achievement continues to decline and costs continue to rise. Delay will only result in legislative controls instituted by further haphazard laws enacted at public demand. Without drastic changes in teacher training, the survival of public education is in immediate jeopardy. Massive reform cannot wait.

Tempest Over Tenure

During the past thirty years, public education has emerged as the one institution that shoulders the major burden of transmitting knowledge, values, and cultures which form our national heritage. Public schools play a major role in social change. Jobs of educators, therefore, just cannot be up for grabs "any old time."

Legislators have sought to protect educators by tenure laws or "fair dismissal codes," and against arbitrary actions on the part of administrators, boards of education, and a community's citizens. Such legislation attempts to ensure an educator's freedom to teach those students who seek to learn. Dismissal codes require boards to follow prescribed procedures relating to longevity, continuing employment, or termination status. Such legal protection is comparable to Civil Service regulations designed to safeguard other public employee groups. Unlike Civil Service procedures requiring merit examinations for appointment, educators must possess college degrees, and specialized credentials to qualify for employment. Boards of education are restricted in the employment of educators by state certification laws. Once employed, both Civil Service workers and public educators enjoy specific, legally insured job security.

Forty-six states and the District of Columbia operate their schools under some form of tenure statute. Continuing contract status is granted following successful completion, usually of a three year probationary period. In spite of widespread opposition by the *American Federation of Teachers* and the *National Education Association*, New York laws have extended the probationary period to five years. Peculiar to education, the continuing contract status is applicable only to the district where it was gained. If a tenured educator resigns to accept a position in another district, even within the state, he forfeits his permanent status and reverts to probationary service. Each district controls and evaluates the quality of service of its own staff members.

Today, tenure is under bitter attack. Most opposition comes from school boards, administrators, and citizen groups. Criticism has been voiced by advocates of educational reform. Political pessures on state legislators to repeal tenure statutes reflect the public's opposition. Even state commissions report that tenure should be abolished.

Opposition to tenure is based on a variety of reasons, some of which are legitimate, others emotional. All require comparisons of professional educators with labor groups in both the private and public sectors. Some criticism usually points to an inadequate probationary period. Others claim tenure grants educators permanent job security.

While tenure itself has weaknesses, the sources of the problem can be found in the lack of valid evaluation instruments. Revised tenure laws, requiring a thorough evaluation process supported by proper dismissal procedures, would protect the competent and provide for removal of the incompetent.

Teacher evaluation, however described, is not always a simple procedure. Nor is it easy to obtain data by which to hold an individual, group, or organization accountable for certain expected results. Appraisal of operations and programs is also elusive.

Accountability is a relatively new concept in educational literature and practice, although the original idea dates back to the biblical account of the fall of man. Everyone is responsible to someone for his actions. The history of mankind is filled with illustrations that all workers, no matter what their title or rank, have always been measured by some employer who holds them accountable.

In the past, public educators were not blamed for poor learning results. The responsibility was placed on the students and parents. But the concept of accountability relating to the success of the school system and its personnel to assure student achievement is a product of the 1970s.

That responsibility to operate the public schools requires delegation of authority is a truism. When a person is charged with some function, he is automatically empowered to carry out the specific tasks required. School responsibility cannot exist without authority. If a person is assigned to do a job, he must be granted appropriate authority to carry it out. Evaluation of public educators is comprised of a twofold process. Consideration must be given to the nature of the assignment, as well as to the ability, training, and experience of the person assigned, before any valid system of appraisal can be effective. The quadrilevel finger of accountability points to state law, the local board, the administration, and the staff. All play an important role in the evaluation of public educators. A breakdown in any one area leads to the destruction of the entire process.

Traditional employee evaluation forms are meaningless. With vague conclusions, few recommendations for specific improvements, and complete lack of standards, these forms represent the epitome of arbitrary and subjective appraisal of teaching personnel. In few cases does employee evaluation ever refer to the *quality* of performance, success of the program, or learning achievements of the students.

One of the most comprehensive evaluation laws has been enacted in California. Known as the *Stull-Rodda Bill*, this act became the first legislation to require that the competence of all certified employees be measured in direct relationship to student achievement. The law, a part of the education code, mandates that each school district board of education conduct evaluation by the following criteria:

1. Establishment of standards of expected student progress in each area of study, and methods for assessing such progress.

2. Assessment of all certificated personnel in relation to the standards of expected student progress.

3. Assessment of all certificated personnel in their performance of other duties adjunct to their regular assignments.

4. Assessment of their effectiveness in maintaining control and preserving a suitable learning environment.

If a certificated employee's performance does not measure up to the particular standards prescribed by the board in any of these four areas, he must be informed in writing, including specific recommendations indicating how he may improve his performance. The state law also requires that administrative assistance be given the employee. Charges that might lead to dismissal for incompetence or unprofessional conduct must be a part of the actual evaluation report.

Many state codes require a board to give an educator advance notice of deficiencies and the opportunity to make corrections before formal charges are made against the person. Some statutes stipulate that an employee receive written charges and a hearing prior to dismissal or demotion. Usually the hearing will be before the board, with the right of appeal to a state administrative agency or the Courts.

It is not the law, board policy, chain of command, nor even the evaluation process that causes employees to become uneasy, disgruntled, or angry. The problem lies in the inability to construct objective standards on which to base the evaluation of an employee. Criteria are subjective and conducive to misleading and inaccurate appraisal. Excluding the teaching of the basic three R's, which are usually taught in the lower elementary grades, more than ninety percent of all school functions elude objective standards of measurement.

Part 2

Death Knell for the Public Schools

8

Crime and Punishment

Many are the theories of ways to teach and learn. They may originate in wild speculation, considered opinion, or deep thought. Theories, however, must be put to the test to be proved good or bad.

Theory, born out of verification of accepted beliefs based on observation and experimentation, becomes valid. It is the guide for change by which we can expect to achieve desired results. Yet even this expectation can be thwarted. It is within the context of conflicting theories that we seek to uncover the failures that beset the public schools.

One reason public education is viewed with outright suspicion is because its formal process appears to breed hundreds of opposing ideals out of the conflict of various methods and goals. Because the act of education deals directly with individuals, teachers, and learners, no predetermined theories, methods, or goals are truly applicable to each one on an equal basis. Observation and experimentation may prove the law of gravity, but those same principles are most difficult to apply to individuals who are each unique.

When someone considers the statement, "People have an unbounded faith in public education, but they distrust the results of the schools," he is immediately confronted with a basic conflict in philosophies. Acceptance of "faith" requires support of schools and educators. "Distrust" demonstrates condemnation of the methods, goals, and results. On the one hand, educators must be thankful for public support. On the other, they should re-examine "distrusted" current goals and practices.

Public Demands Discipline

The need for public schools is generally supported, but today's public wrath, directed at educators, expresses disenchantment with a failing system. It is charged that the system refuses to recognize its own professional corruptive practices. The public sings the blues, but educators turn a deaf ear. People demand education and will support a particular system as long as results are acceptable. But the taxpayer's mood makes him ready to intervene directly into actual school operation. Citizen groups have captured the initiative in the battle for control of public education.

The public believes poor teachers remain in the classrooms. Yet it is hesitant to support programs of research to develop valid standards for personnel evaluation. Few people seek practical solutions to upgrade, modify, or change the entire basis for evaluation, for somehow, the whole concept of educational measurement, evaluation, or standards is equated with school discipline. Citizen groups are deeply angered by laxity in discipline. The groups feel the discipline problem can be blamed for a generation of unlearned and violent rebels who stand against the very society in which they should be educated to find a place. Public criticism is rooted in disgust, fear, anger, and frustration over violence, which the schools do not, or cannot, control.

Students, teachers, and administrators report startling descriptions of prevailing conditions in public schools. Elected lawmakers, judicial officials, and the public listen with growing indignation. All call for concerted action to solve the problem.

Statistics, backed by scores of national investigations, indicate junior and senior high schools are riddled by drug abuse and student violence to the degree that teaching and learning have been replaced by the effort just to survive. Juvenile delinquency has touched the lives of a majority of students. In alarming reports given congressmen, it is noted that:

1. More than ninety percent of the students enrolled in one Ohio school are known to have been on drugs for more than one-half of each term in one school year.

2. A police crackdown on one campus in a rural Missouri school of 700 students uncovered nearly two truckloads of deadly weapons (ranging from guns and knives to bombs and blackjacks) on the persons of students present on one normal day at school.

3. One metropolitan system in California has records that reveal more than 300 physical assaults on staff members during just one eight-week period.

Under such conditions, it is impossible to teach and to learn. Personal safety is placed above the purpose of the school. Bored students claim the schools fail to meet their needs. When they turn on to drugs and violent acts, they are either expelled or drop out. The tragic failure in modern society is that drugs and open violence in the schools are part of the American heritage.

Who's to Blame?

The public has been warned that one national education union intends to usurp the legal and administrative controls now held by legislative representatives. For ten years, it has alerted the public to the latent force commanded by educators in the traditional political process.

A recent union president has stated: ". . . Teachers form the largest single political striking force in the entire country. They are determined to control the purse strings of the schools to enable them to bypass local boards of education . . . Teachers will then have the power to set the direction of education . . ." Most of this union's members truly believe their collective strength will permit them to control school operations, management, and local boards.

One of the first stated objectives of this organization is to eliminate teacher responsibility and accountability for student discipline. This task is to be forced on school administrators. A prominent eastern teacher union leader was recently quoted as saying, ". . . And if administrators cannot handle student discipline to stop the drug, violent, and criminal behavior of problem students, we will have the power and authority to have them fired . . ."

Surely it should be realized that the administrative group, numbering no more than two or three at elementary level, perhaps three or four at junior high school level, and only four or five at the secondary level, will never be able to control the discipline of student bodies ranging in size from 1,000 to 4,000 students per school.

Community pressure will force boards of education to consider alternatives. They could return the disciplinary function to the teachers as part of their contracted job description. Legally, this would require teachers either to be responsible or to be fired. With collective bargaining laws in effect, communities could expect teachers to walk out over "intolerable" working conditions. In a concerted effort to amend laws to make legal responsibility for student discipline an administrative function, teachers could strike on a statewide basis. Should such notions cause amendments, a huge increase in school administrative costs can be expected.

A board might consider another way to control anti-social behavior. Students given to excessive truancy and disruptive actions could be remanded to parental control.

A third option would be to call for increase in police control. This would ultimately create a prisonlike school system, and would be a radical way to control the student. But some metropolitan areas have resorted to planting under-cover police agents to spy on students. Some citizen groups consider this form of infiltration a violation of individual rights.

One California school board adopted regulations to pre-vent police from masquerading as students when they at-tempted to uncover drug offenders, pushers, and criminals on campus. Board action was prompted by mass arrests, alleged injustice, and reported disruption of the school pro-gram. The board felt that undercover police action would create suspicion among students, parents, and the commu-nity. Rational citizens, as well as educators, look to the total society to help the students return to their once proud status as citadels of learning. But the statistics of many opinion polls support stronger school discipline. Many a citizen believes that improvement of public education is possible only with an appropriate use of police force in support of educators, parents, and the courts.

State and national surveys reflect the seriousness of this school problem. Highlights of several polls conducted in one western state reveal the following facts:

1. Elementary schools rate high on achieve-ment only through the fifth grade level.

2. More than 50 percent of those responding rated high school discipline as nonexistent.

3.   The public is unanimous in open condemnation of the school counseling services.

4.   Over 70 percent favor the use of police to eliminate drugs from the public schools.

5.   More than 80 percent demand expulsion of disruptive students so interested students may enjoy acceptable conditions.

Punishment Goes to Court

Until recent times, disciplinary action was based on a school official's role *in loco parentis;* the official acted in the legal stead of the parent. Public educators determined the rules of conduct in the name of the parents. In no case did constitutional rights become an issue of civil contention. Violators of the rules were subject to immediate disciplinary measures appropriate to the situation. But times have changed.

Two recent Supreme Court decisions show us the modern problem. In *Goss v. Lopez,* the high court held that any student suspension or expulsion of even short duration involved consitutional rights of those affected. The decision declared that *due process,* in the form of some kind of notice and hearing prior to suspension or expulsion, is required before deprivation of rights may be carried out by school officials. In *Wood v. Strickland,* the court ruling narrowed the scope of immunity from personal liability normally held by elected officials. Under the provisions of the *Civil Rights Act* of 1871, a board of education member was exempted from personal liability *unless* he acted with malice, hatred, and ill will. By the terms of the *Wood* decision, an elected officeholder may

> . . . be acting sincerely . . . but an act involving a student's constitutional rights can no more be justified by ignorance on the part of the one entrusted with supervision of students than by the presence of actual malice . . .

The consequences of these two decisions impose a constitutional *doctrine of fairness* on public educators. Such has never before been known. All school administrators now know that policies and regulation must provide *due process* in all cases of suspension or expulsion. But the ramifications of individual liability are not yet known. Of course, board members, administrators, and teachers may also seek *due process* in civil suits dealing with charges brought against them.

Court rulings on the constitutional rights of students are confused, thereby confusing school administrators, who do not understand just what disciplinary measures may or may not apply. They cannot assume that *due process* prevents immediate and appropriate action, including expulsion.

A landmark decision, *Tinker v. Des Moines Independent School District (395 US 503-512)*, created a further substantial body of case law upholding the right of school authorities to expel unruly students:

Any conduct, in class or out of it, which for any reason . . . whether it may stem from time, place or type of behavior . . . materially disrupts classwork or involves substantial disorder . . . is not immunized by the constitutional guaranty of freedom of speech . . .

This decision backs immediate and affirmative administrative action to maintain school control. Administrators must act in keeping with the spirit of *due process*, but do possess lawful means to apply reasonable discipline, including expulsion.

School officials must be willing to

1. Adopt reasonable rules for student behavior with valid participation of students, teachers, parents, and citizens.

2. Publish and disseminate specific rules of conduct applicable to all students which aree made known to parents and citizens.

3. Adopt policies that hold all educators accountable for uniform enforcement of the rules.

4. Bring written charges against students for specific infraction, in which all involved are informed of their legal rights to counsel at least ten school days before holding a hearing.

5. Hold a legitimate hearing, at which time a student is permitted to examine all evidence and question witnesses.

6. Provide the student and his parents with a written decision.

Enforcement of school regulations, in keeping with known legal restraints, can restore order by eliminating disruptive students. Only then can the system claim an atmosphere conducive to learning. Educators and community leaders must understand the conflict in the act of student expulsion. The system seeks to retain its student in school, yet its administrators know that the disruptive cannot be allowed to remain and to curtail learning opportunities.

School finance enters the picture, too. One school district in an affluent Pennsylvania area reported a ten percent loss in State revenue due to expulsion and absences. Another system in upstate New York suffered an absence rate of nearly thirty days per semester by well over one-half the student body. In a school district in Illinois more than eighty percent of all known school violence involved students with chronically poor attendance records. One large California district absorbed a loss of over $2 million in support funds because of student absences. None of these figures accounts for the costs of school vandalism and property damage caused by student violence.

Everyone must be concerned about the cost of paying to support new and separate institutions to care for expelled students. Most people understand that any lasting solution to violence, absenteeism, and drug abuse is not found in multiplication of additional public agencies. The criminal element cannot be removed from the jurisdiction of one institution and placed under the custody of another without a corresponding increase in expenditure of tax funds.

Compulsory Attendance

Since 1852, when they became a legislative reality in Massachusetts, laws have demanded compulsory school attendance. The traditional notion that instruction was an obligation of the family was long gone. Compulsory schooling became the law of the land in this evolutionary process. Government wielded the legal power and authority to compel parents to send their children to school. Enforcement is now carried out in all states. Society has been granted no alternative; parents are required to have their children educated in some type of institution. The only option is the parental freedom to select what kind. All boys and girls must be enrolled in either a public system or a private school. This is the solitary choice.

Those who are content with school attendance laws, without thought or question, send their children to public schools. Others resent governmental coercion and seek the alternative of private school. It is a fact of modern economic life that millions of people cannot afford tuition fees. They have no choice at all. Those who reject both kinds of schooling are frustrated, angry citizens who represent a growing group which seeks sweeping changes in the system. Those demands relate to certain questions which someone must resolve:

1. Do citizens merely seek to abolish compulsory attendance laws in favor of voluntary enrollment?

2. Do the demands for change mean that society approves a lowering of the age for compulsory attendance?

3. Is public frustration vented to force needed changes in the school curricula?

4. Do the demands for change refer to elimination of school crime and violence which negates real learning?

Answers to these questions rightly present a challenge to professional leaders charged with directing the future of education. Each question implies concern over the wisdom of any compulsory system. Sound research into both our schools and our society must answer the challenge, for both will be affected greatly by decisions setting educational directions.

Many child labor laws have been enacted coincidentally with compulsory attendance regulations. None was enforced consistently until after World War II. During the past thirty years, the primary intent of compulsory school attendance would seem to be to control the labor force rather than to provide education for all.

The ability to read, write, and understand arithmetic is absolutely necessary for a person to survive in modern society, and millions of jobs exist that require little more than these basic skills. But many job opportunities remain hidden from public view because employers expect and require applicants to possess a completion of high school certificate. School dropouts are unemployed simply because they can neither meet the age nor the school requirements imposed upon them by a society proud of its technological stature.

The labor market entrance requirement is a type of learning situation itself. It has become a social means to direct youth to raise its own occupational sights. In effect, taxpayers are providing opportunities for boys and girls to improve their skills before they reach the labor market. This same expenditure of public funds could just as well be used for educational programs to improve necessary skills on the job, *after* youth has entered the labor force. It would then have more meaning for those enrolled because they would be participating on a voluntary basis.

Society has expected the schools to provide training for personal, social, and vocational demands. But that which education does for an individual may not always meet the demands for needs of society. Conversely, school programs designed to meet expected social requirements may not be acceptable to those enrolled. Ideals of the adult generation are often in direct conflict with desires of the young. The public schools have always been a kind of "no man's land," a stopgap measure to interrupt the collision course between the two generations.

Young people are not exactly alike in abilities, interests, and aspirations. Advancing through the successive grade levels, students reach, in their own good time, their own distinct uniqueness. Some are ready for entry into the adult world of jobs, marriage, and family obligations. Others need further training in the basic and vocational skills.

Most students are resigned to peer, teacher, or parental pressures, and play a game called "preparation for further training in college." They know that public schools force secondary students to accept a curricular pattern with little variation.

If high school experience is supposed to equip graduates with necessary skills required by the work world, then the entire system must be reexamined immediately. Many findings show conclusively that a four year block of courses, no matter how they may be labeled or divided, is neither necessary nor suitable for all students.

The public is convinced that educators have failed to distinguish differences in achievement between students who complete the required courses for normal graduation and those who reach the same level of accomplishment at the ninth grade level. If no identifiable marks of superiority exist, then the only difference the school makes is that 12th grade students are four years older. The high school becomes not a place for learning, but only a tax-supported place for pastimes, a place where students can be kept off the labor market until they have reached the age of majority.

Taking Care of the Dropout

Enforcement of school attendance laws, resting on parental cooperation, is far from effective. A daily attendance rate of less than 75 percent in some schools is not unusual. In other high schools, the same number of students are absent as are present. These days, benign neglect seems to have replaced enforcement. The lack of parental cooperation, coupled with the severity of problems beyond the age of 14, has called into question the high costs of attendance enforcement.

Few critics offer any workable solutions, although agreement that compulsory attendance procedures must be modified appears unanimous. The reasons popularly advanced are:

1. Students are forcibly subjected to a deceitful and violent school environment.

2. An awesome boredom has resulted from poor student attitudes and worthless courses in the name of innovation.

3. The system has failed to provide alternatives in a complex society.

The *National Committee on Reform of Secondary Education (ROSE)* has recommended lowering the compulsory school age to 14 years. The report concludes:

This nation does not need laws that force adolescents to
go to school [beyond] age 14 . . . . It requires schools and
programs which make them wish to attend . . .

The act of modifying age requirements to eliminate
dropout students is questionable. The adult lives of millions
of boys and girls could be damaged. It is certain that, out of
school, youth will not remain idle. Those who find jobs will
enter society in an acceptable manner. But what of those who
remain unemployed? They will be forced to choose between
joining the welfare rolls or turning to criminal activities. In
either case, society will suffer the unhappy consequences.

Public schools have now been placed in the untenable
position of being forced to develop alternative and incentive
programs acceptable to the students. The charge is to induce
the dropout to return to some form of learning activity. The
thrust of the future is toward education offered as a voluntary, lifelong, essential ingredient of human survival.

If the secondary schools are to escape a regrettable fate
as custodial institutions, the states must undertake legislative
action to relieve educators of the enforcement function. A
model of one statutory revision is patterned after the existing
code in one state.

All parents, guardians and other persons in this State having custody of any minor child shall cause such child to
attend either the public schools of the district in which
the child resides for the full terms of the school year or to
attend a private school for the identical session. Excep-
tions to the provisions of this Code may be made by the
local district superintendent when he determines that a
child is physically or mentally unable to attend school or
has already attained the equivalent proficiency in the
common subjects required by law to be taught in the first
eight grades of the public schools of this State or the child
is regularly and lawfully employed in useful, legitimate,
and remunerative occupation, or the child has received a
certificate of educational competence from any school
established under Code regulations as carried out by the

State Board of Education through each local district superintendent.

Acceptance of the fact that effective learning cannot always be engendered by compulsory attendance laws will be a first step toward eliminating the dilemma educators face.

9

Equal Opportunity and Finances

Court-ordered integration of students enrolled in the public schools has failed to create any viable measure of equality of educational opportunities. Nor are further judicial mandates likely to be any more successful. National statistics provide a gloomy outlook for any busing or boundary-line attempt at successful enforcing of integration in community schools. Enforcement is distasteful to the student and parent alike.

Busing of students across political and racial boundaries is not the most efficient method by which to provide equal educational opportunities. Yet, court-ordered busing of students has become an inflexible tool to prod the school system.

It is evident that desegregation is effective only when school officials can harness cooperation of all governmental bodies at the local, state, and national levels. Total commitment to a new type of communications exchange program has to underscore a broadside attempt to alleviate legitimate fear about the long-range consequences of integrated schools. A troubled public cannot be expected to support a social experiment until it is shown that there will first be a decrease in crime and violence in the schools.

A belief is held that reduction in the size of mammoth school districts would make education a more personal experience for both students and parents, and would encourage public involvement. It is also believed that an acceptable degree of integration would result because of the closer relationships in a small district.

School district bigness does contribute greatly to the problems of desegregation, and all of the many related concerns of attendance, discipline, and rebellion. Smaller districts seem much less affected because school-community relations are carried out at a more personal level. Once the intimate involvement of the community in school affairs has been lost, educational problems leap. Parents feel they do not control the destiny of their children in giant districts. Signs of community withdrawal from support of the schools may be found wherever crime and violence reign. In those areas of strictly segregated race, attitudes of public support are at cross-purposes. It is time to create local units for school operation within the larger districts where no need will be felt to increase segregation nor force desegregation.

Social justice before the law cannot become reality until equality of educational opportunity is available to all, regardless of social, ethnic, or economic status. Improvement in school programs could create the one social institution where forces of discontent, injustice, and inequality would be eliminated. Indeed, a democratic society has no acceptable alternative.

The Hand Is Out

Federal aid to public education has long been considered the logical solution to school financing problems. Schools have always received federal money throughout their history, although most federal aid is granted to support categorical programs. This means a local district may receive funds for a specific purpose, with the programs usually administered through a host of federal agencies.

Objections to federal control and lack of coordination among the many federal programs always come with categorial aid funds. But school officials regret the minimum level of federal support. Although federal aid has increased during the last decade, the overall amount is only a fraction of public school costs. No matter how much federal aid a district receives from the state or national governments, the differential in ability of local areas to support public education still persists.

Obviously, financial limitation exercises far more control in poor districts than in wealthy areas. In one rural Michigan school district, a survey showed that provisions for school libraries, programs for gifted and handicapped students, and art and music classes were all but nonexistent. Such variation in the availability of school tax funds has produced current inequities in most educational programs.

Conclusions of many studies, conducted by a host of blue ribbon communities at state and national levels, have all underscored problems of irresponsible school funding methods. Increased judicial action indicates concern over impending school financial collapse. Recent court decisions repeatedly point out the chronic inequity of traditional tax procedures.

Several states have taken steps to reform their school financing systems, but the efforts are still in the judicial and legislative states. Some landmark legislation has been enacted in an effort to create fairness to taxpayers by the provision of equal educational opportunities. But those laws have yet to be placed into effect.

During the past twenty years, state aid programs have been expanded in an effort to strengthen local districts. In many cases, state aid has proved to be the only way to equalize school funding and keep local control. The alternative would be to transfer control of the schools to county, regional, state, or national government.

Unless workable solutions to the school finance problems can be found, school control will more and more be removed from the local community. These are legitimate fears of people who want to retain some control over the educational destiny of their children. Expansion of state aid will change traditional problems in school financing; low wealth districts will receive increased funds. But additional revenue will bring new controls. Results can be disastrous, for community desire for educational improvement may be eradicated by state effort, an effort that can only decrease public participation in school affairs.

State efforts to enact laws that will shift the school tax burden from real property to some other type of base are usually attached to pending bills to provide relief of the total tax obligation, bound to be favored by voters. But revenues lost from tax reduction in one area must be regained from tax increases in another. If the total amount of taxes collected falls, all areas of public services have to be curtailed. School tax reform measures, add-on riders to bills, are indications of the role politics plays in school tax legislation.

A conflict of values exists in every aspect of educational financing. People disagree on most issues relating to school finance. They seek different means to achieve different ends. In school tax elections, nearly two-thirds of parents of school age children have traditionally voted for an increase in taxes to improve the programs. The elderly and owners of rental properties have voted in like proportions for low taxes. All people want good schools, but they are not all equally dedicated in their desire to pay for them.

Immediate reform of the school tax-finance laws is essential to our nation. No longer should the social destiny of any American youth be destined by or be dependent upon the accident of his or her place of birth. It is time to end inequality of educational opportunities in the public school system.

10

The Battle
Is Joined

The greatest single hurdle educators must face is the lack of public confidence in those who operate the school system. Degeneration of the image provided by measured learning achievement is a shameful accusation by taxpayers. The public now believes the schools to be grossly negligent and incapable of their mission to educate boys and girls.

Concerned parents know, too, that they have been eased out of sincere participation in school operation. They probe for the issues around which to muster all forces. The public at large seeks to gain total control of the school system.

A Predictable Collapse

The problems of public education are particularly acute in urban areas. Violence in the street has bloomed into rebellion in the classroom. A growing problem of society has become an outright menace to the public schools. Crime in the central city schools grows like a suffocating vine.

In many areas, literally thousands of students have no interest in learning. They roam halls, bang lockers, disrupt classes, and foment trouble. Reports in both slum-ridden and affluent suburban areas all reveal a growing anxiety among teachers, counselors, administrators, and the public toward young offenders. Most authorities predict this concern will spread to the rural areas, if, indeed, it has not already. Unless operated on, schools will be consumed by the dreadful social cancer that today permeates society.

One state superintendent of public education has stated, "Our public schools are not working; the system is actually blowing apart at the seams."

A former superintendent of an eastern metropolitan district has warned, "Urban education is on the very edge of collapse."

The president of a teachers' association in one western state has predicted, "Unless legislative action is forthcoming to provide effective controls over this disruptive group, public education will become intolerable and nonexistent within five years."

Teachers have been physically attacked in their classrooms, administrators assaulted in their offices. A superintendent was murdered in his downtown administrative complex. Students often confront their own classmates in brutal fights in school halls.

The public agrees there is a problem, but it is divided on how to solve it—as are school administrators. Legislators brand the gloomy predictions as extreme. Judges refuse to heed the warnings. Teachers are caught on the hook of responsibility for school crime. Most school people remain mute while the situation grows daily more tragic.

While leaders of citizens groups and parents urge an end to a general permissiveness, no group looks beyond the schools for the roots of violence. Educators are blamed for a problem beyond their legal capacity to control.

The cost of teenage crime is increasing alarmingly. Many states spend more money to incarcerate a youth than they do to provide him with a useful education. In one state, over $10,000 per year is spent to care for one student. In the same year, this state spent less than $800 per pupil per year for public education. Such disparities in expenditures represent a shortsighted and meaningless attempt to evade the responsibilities of society to educate its children. Expenditure of funds ever reaches for the causes of school violence. We can expect an ever-increasing tax bill to curtail crime by the young.

Rebellion against the schools may erupt merely out of frustration. A high school in a western state was broken into by three boys who "had nothing to do." They systematically destroyed the television shop to the tune of $100,000. These same boys set fire to a school library located some 50 miles from their home area. Under questioning, none offered any reason except hatred for the schools. Total damages for those two escapades by just three boys amounted to more than $5 million. Each dollar spent on repairs, new buildings, and replacement of equipment is one dollar less for books, machines, and more teachers.

The damages go far beyond property reduced to ashes. In the one case, shop classes were cancelled, and hundreds of students were denied the opportunity to learn. In the latter case, the entire high school student body continued class work without necessary materials.

The public has been told that troublemakers represent a minority. When the majority makes no effort to stop the havoc, are not all a part of rebellion against the system? Read these typical examples:

   1.   A teacher was killed in the classroom by a bullet which richocheted off the wall. The sixteen-year-old boy waved the gun around in full view of the entire class for several minutes before the shot. Police records indicated he had been arrested twice

before for armed robbery. When questioned, he claimed he shot at a dog which had just then wandered into the classroom.

2.   The morning bus ride to school degenerated into a light-up time for the marijuana gang. No bus driver, facing odds of seventy-five to one, is about to intervene. So, in full view of the innocent friends, the pot bunch floats to class in no condition to learn.

3.   Unruly boys stuff paper wads into ceiling sprinklers before lighting them with a match. Students jump back to their seats when the teacher enters the room. They giggle with glee when the sprinklers turn on to flood the classroom.

4.   Bullies stand guard at a classroom door as a couple have sexual intercourse inside. As their classmates appear, they are charged a quarter to enter and see the show. When the teacher arrives, the door is locked and the keyhole stuffed with wire. No one can enter the room.

Such episodes represent the wave of campus violence, vandalism, and rebellion that has educators across the nation calling for legal action. School boards have been persuaded to employ a school police force to patrol the halls. Others have erected barbed wire fences to replace the open campus. Only a few understand that the roots of student rebellion go too deep for punitive action against the total school population.

School problems are affecting more and more students who simply mirror the social conditions in which they live. As violence, crime, and rebellion erupts in the adult community, so they increase in the schools. Most educators would agree that campus problems are an extension of widespread social unrest.

Philosophical Disparities

The public does not operate the schools; it elects a board of education to represent its interests. Professional educators do not set policy; they administer programs to achieve what the public expects. The public formulates policy—either through law or legal codes—and the professionals carry out the decisions.

Disparities in this democratic cooperation arise when one group fails to communicate with the other the problems that prevent success. The public expects students to learn, but educators must have conditions that make possible the teaching-learning process. School failure is the result of a breakdown in understanding between the legally constituted public policy-makers and professional educators.

Legislative efforts to modify compulsory attendance laws have circumvented public will by lowering standards traditionally required for a high school diploma. Neither the public nor the educators understand the full impact. New laws actually make the sixteen-year-old eligible to take a special examination. If he passes, he will be granted a certificate equivalent to a diploma.

Replacing compulsory attendance laws with laws allowing evidence of proficiency by examination will produce cumulative effects such as the following:

1. Elimination of the eleventh and twelfth grades for up to fifty percent of the student body.

2. Reduction of the value of a diploma to nothing more than the completion of a one-hour examination.

3. Cut school expenditures in like proportion to the number of students leaving school upon receipt of a proficiency certificate.

4. Enlargement of the American work force
with millions of youth who possess minimal educational skills evidenced only by a written test.

Laws relating to proficiency certificates have been enacted to reduce the absence rates of upper grade students.
The early graduation program lops off the two years of traditional high school. In reality, tenth grade students could be
considered seniors in the schools of the future.

But most surveys of teachers, parents, and business
people reveal solid opposition to this reform. All groups
deplore the intent of a law that lowers school standards.
They believe they have been deceived by the lawmakers. It is
felt that more effort should have been made to improve existing programs. Nearly ninety percent of people questioned
in one survey believed that such laws undermined parental
control over local school's authority to determine graduation
requirements.

Lack of discipline goes hand in hand with the dropout
problem. Administrators have devised procedures to keep
students attending classes, but only when they so choose
under individual instruction. They have made class time flexible and nonstructured. Some courses are relabeled, have no
requirements, and do not give grades. Seminars are held on
student-selected topics; field trips are taken in student-
operated cars; community projects are created and regular
doses of films are administered.

Evaluation of student achievement is based on contracts
made between teacher and student, resting solely upon
attendance. Units of credit are assigned upon completion of
"seat time" spent in these programs. Courses can be one week
long or last for the entire semester. "Alternative education" is
directed toward keeping students in school. An acceptable
standard of accomplishment is not a requirement.

Without standards or grades to represent achievement,
no one stands accountable for anything. The administration

provides attendance statistics for the collection of state money according to the average daily attendance. The teacher acts as a baby-sitter without inspiration to teach because students' marks are not computed. The student attends those classes he selects because he knows he will be passed along. Because the student is off the streets, the parents accept the program. The end result is a loss of interest in learning. Tardiness, truancy, and class-cutting are commonplace. Yet, students are maintained on the rolls so that the school system may receive state income.

These advancement without achievement policies have brought havoc to three generations of students. Many graduates have entered society as functional illiterates. Governmental and business surveys have placed the figure as high as five million youth who cannot perform basic skills on a fifth grade proficiency level. No one is able to project the long-range loss and effect on the national economy. But those truly concerned can only shudder in frustration at these practices.

Nearly every public opinion indicates that people are against educational frills, academic innovations, and the lack of standards. Most surveys also indicate a demand for schools to return to basic and fundamental studies taught to standards of achievement without social promotion. Adults are insisting upon a new type of accountability for every institution funded by tax money. Parents intend to have crime and violence removed from the schools to allow the majority of willing students learn the skills necessary for them to compete in adult society.

Educators know the decline in the national scores on the *Scholastic Aptitude Tests*. But teachers and administrators have refused to equate the deemphasis on educational standards and emphasis on social promotion with decreasing achievement. The claim is made that the tests do not measure what has been taught. Educators insist that no accountability can be applied to them when the very system for which they work is unable to maintain order and enforce rules of attendance.

Dedicated educators consider absenteeism as a lost opportunity for the teacher to instruct and the student to learn. Laws and practices partly offset this by providing home teachers and longer times for completion of work when student absences are due to legitimate illness.

Truancy remains the unresolved catastrophe. No accountability can be demanded of educators for student learning if students refuse to attend classes. Class attendance is a direct responsibility of parents in particular and society in general.

Factors other than simple truancy contributing to student absenteeism are family attitudes, social pressures from environmental peer groups, economic circumstances, and a general breakdown in court enforcement of existing attendance laws. Since these are often discounted, it is little wonder that a national commission now urges a lowering of the compulsory attendance age to fourteen years or the completion of the eighth grade. (Most states require youth to attend school until they reach the age of eighteen.) The commission report concludes, ". . . Coercion of compulsory attendance is no longer working and the states should return the problem of school attendance to the parents, who remain legally responsible . . ."

The incentive to redesign secondary education continues through the relentless release of many national reports. One such report, issued by ROSE (the National Committee on Reform of Secondary Education), supports a wide range of recommendations of alternative types of schooling. It recommends overhaul of the curriculum under an expansion of student rights, a ban on all forms of corporal punishment, and the elimination of sexism and racial bias. Its major point is the abolition of compulsory attendance laws. The schools can no longer remain custodial institutions, the report states, adding, "The harm done to the schools by students who do not wish to learn is measured not only by vandalism, assault and theft, but by the subtle degradation of the general tone of the system . . . ."

Such an admission denies educators' accountability, which can become a reality only through the cooperation of every socially responsible member of society.

It's All in the Family

The basis of every community is the family—the primary unit that determines community direction and purpose, the cohesive group that shapes the initial physical, mental, spiritual, and social character of each individual. Its survival depends partly upon its relationship with the group of families constituting the neighborhood. Here school values enter to affect the lives of children enrolled in the schools. The adjustment between family control and school authority is the foundation for local determination of the public schools. Neighborhood and community unity must be maintained by concerted and cooperative support for and control of the local schools. Any disintegration of that relationship undermines the very foundation of modern society. This is the crux in the struggle for control of public education.

A *National Committee for Citizens in Education* (NCCE) was formed to lead and direct local community groups in their demand for school improvement. In an effort to gather information about parental concerns, this committee established a direct telephone "hot line." Anyone irate over school problems was invited to call. The NCCE was able to catalog major issues, as well as provide the caller with information on practices in other areas.

This toll free liaison provided the first national attempt to formulate a workable and immediate program of public information about reading, discipline, and academic ratings to curriculum, pupil safety, and budget control. Answers, suggestions, and recommendations were given each caller. Aided by a Ford Foundation grant, the NCCE functioned to coordinate citizen group participation in school affairs. The goal was to redress the imbalance between the public and professional educators.

The sheer size of administrative organizations has created a huge barrier that makes impossible local citizen participation in the establishment of educational policies. Parents have no real understanding of the preparation of complex school budgets. Nor do they know how to evaluate existing programs to determine for themselves if they are receiving true measure for dollars spent.

People cannot build a better community except by improving their schools. Since most people find themselves unable to live outside community solidarity, they must strive to create neighborhoods with values acceptable to the majority. There is absolutely no room for public apathy.

Educators must solicit citizen support of the schools. They must try to understand the sources of public frustration. They are obliged to open the records and discuss every criticism. Most of all, educators must heed the message of people alarmed at school issues. Cooperation is the key.

Control of school policy belongs ultimately to the people rather than to professional educators. Determination of methods rightfully should be delegated to a staff, but the public may well reserve the right to dictate the purpose, direction, and extent of all programs. And surely the public deserves an accounting of results.

Divergence of opinion between professional and layman over the curricula has been a festering social ill since the second century. Here is a translation of an 1800-year-old blast by Roman satirist Petronius, made in 162 A.D. The statement is in *The Satyricon:*

> We fail to teach our children; we merely lull them to sleep and then release them into our world as half-baked . . . . Our schools keep them utterly ignorant of real life, which remains an experience they never see or feel . . . . All

they learn are the scribbling edicts of tyrants who mumble about condemning virgins to be sacrificed to stop the plague . . . . The results are all the same and the materials they study are comparable to honeyballs, poppyseed and sesame . . . .

Public indignation over a defunct process has surely been intensified throughout successive centuries. Many leaders today level identical charges.

When stripped of camouflage, the community and the school seem separate entities impossible to unite. Each is composed of people with contradictory motives, views, and ideas. They refuse to behave in a neat, statistical, and predictable manner that can be validated by test results and standards achieved.

Measurement of schools, isolated from an evaluation of home and family life, will provide results false to both institutions. The schools will not produce excellence in all youth, but educators who are not required to make surpassing effort to accomplish excellence will never attempt to do that which they *are* able to achieve.

11

The Community Can Win

During the last two generations, public educators have been embroiled in debates with critics of the school system over a multitude of controversial issues. Ringing indictments are heard from those directly involved with or interested in the education of youth. Parents, teachers, and students—all accuse today's system because it cannot or will not reform itself. Many believe that the schools are on the brink of real and total collapse.

Several current polls indicate that elected school officials have dropped in esteem to an all-time low because people consider such leaders as out of touch with local needs. Most Americans seem even unwilling to support educational policies made by local politicians who promise much but deliver little by way of improved schools. A majority indicated distrust of central office, state, and national planning because they provide merely an illusion of true public control that people believe rightfully belongs to local citizens.

Factions do agree on one point: that current fads promising to correct the ills of public schools only camouflage inherent problems. Innovation in curriculum, administrative skills, and business methods bring no permanent solutions. While educators, parents, and lawmakers flounder, attacks on the system and dropouts from it increase.

We hear the cry to turn aside the dead hand of the past and unrealistic traditions. Time-honored and proven procedures, disciplines, and bureaucratic organization must not bind the schools. Many accept the charge that old ethical, social, and academic standards have no place in this modern age of transformation.

The old standards are replaced with varied plans for change in all directions, all designed to lead policy-makers toward viable solutions by the year 2000 A.D. But the revival of the public schools cannot wait in "think-tank" limbo until then. Revolutionary change, for total improvement, is essential now.

Isolated innovation here and there will not work to improve the system overall. Nor will any program of alternative instruction provide new lifeblood. Clever discussion on questions unrelated to standards or values that can be evaluated will produce yet another generation of unprepared and uninformed, but talkative, illiterates. Efforts to change the system based on anything other than research, standards, and measured results, only extends the nightmare of constantly shifting fads, ideas, and values.

A summary list of the real issues is appropriate here.

What Arguments Are About

1. Breakdown in school discipline and compulsory attendance.

2. Inequitable system of funding schools.

3. Failure of programs for special-problem youth.

4. Nonexistent professional counseling for students, parents, and educators.

5. Ineffective communication with the public.

6. No adequate assessment of student progress.

7. Ineffective control over personnel training and evaluation.

8. Lack of cohesion and continuity between educational levels.

9. Watered-down and misused curricular materials.

10. Inability to instruct students to meet acceptable standards.

Renovation of the schools through completely interlocking reform is the sole hope left. The problem of rebuilding, with a planned program of change, should be the prime concern of every faculty member, administrator, board of education, student, parent, and legislator.

A Powerful Political Platform

For more than two hundred years the American public school system has been accepted as the central institution around which the local community revolved to ensure continued identity. Modern reorganization has reduced the number while increasing the size of school districts. The result has been an erosion of the neighborhood pattern of school operation. A community loses its identity as it loses control over its schools.

The breakup of community control mirrors society's breakup of control. Just as the population growth of urban areas has mushroomed, the ever-larger school district has become a highly centralized bureaucracy. There is yet no national stranglehold on public education, but the enlarged school districts already represent a new arm of government.

Each new unification of several small districts spreads the community identity that much thinner. The historic concept of local schools has all but disappeared from the urban-suburban scene. Millions, rather than hundreds, now demand new school policies, revised divisions of grade levels, different course content, and greater emphasis on modernized facilities. But communities are not going down without a fight. People in neighborhoods are banding together to demand decentralization of sprawling school complexes.

Public impetus toward a breakup of large unified school districts will create a highly significant political platform for the next generation. People just naturally fear a system of massive public education in which the seat of control is moved ever further away from the community and the parent.

Local Voices for National Change

Society searches for ways to instruct youth to cope with change. Communities seek to maintain an identity that revolves around the schools. Parents demand a voice in the education of their children through control of their own neighborhood school programs. All citizens expect much from the system. The ever mounting frustrations intensify the demand for a return to community-based local control of the school.

School problems are on a national scale, but solutions will come from people in neighborhood forums. When people become active in local school affairs, they reinforce the concept that community citizens form the very foundation upon which direct and effective improvements may be made in the democractic control of education. The local community is the only place from which acceptable school decisions emerge into actual practice.

Of course, no one overall pattern of education will answer the needs of all people in every hamlet, village, and city across this nation. But the basic principle of our form of government flourishes only within a working relationship of school, child, parent, and educator at the community level. This bond of democratic strength rests upon millions of people in thousands of communities determining the best ways to meet the needs of their own schools. Educational directions set by representatives elected in each neighborhood will reflect national solidarity. Broad participation by community citizens can foster an intelligent responsibility for public school reform, one ensuring state and national interests.

There is no reason to believe citizens in numberless communities throughout the nation will suddenly become experts in school affairs. Nor can they be expected to burst forth with marvelous solutions to the many educational problems. But given their initial interest, people must be encouraged to band together for school improvement by creating an institution locally controlled by representatives of everyone directly affected.

If old neighborhood "Public School #4" could be transformed into a center for community affairs, to be utilized by children, parents, and citizens, it would become the focal point for a broad cross section of community people. The local school must be recognized as a basic neighborhood possession, ready for constant use by every citizen. The community school must become an integral part of local daily activities just as is the corner drugstore, supermarket, or familiar post office.

Today we see a huge increase in power and activity usurped by the state and national governments over the schools. Controls have been removed to central offices ever further from the people closest to schools. The change in once familiar patterns of community pride in neighborhood schools has been a painful experience to millions of adults, but it is a change that can be fought.

The public schools must offer an example of meaningful democratic participation. And with that participation, community controls of the schools can break the stranglehold of a centralized bureaucracy. Public education has no place for remotely based officialdom claiming ultimate power over local school operations.

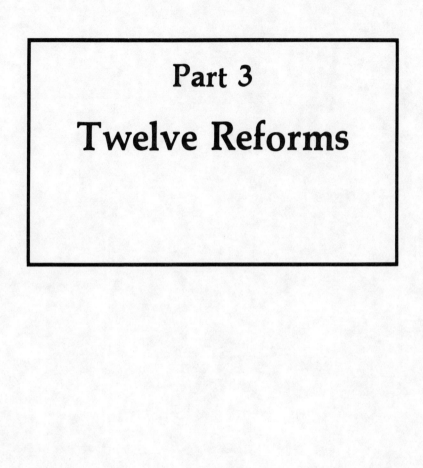

Part 3

Twelve Reforms

12

Eye on the
Local Citizen

If the public school system is ever to serve the student as its initial client, it must be controlled and directed by actively involved community citizens. All other reforms depend squarely upon each community's participation in school and community affairs. Anything less than such involvement means alienation from the system. Nothing short of a complete reorganization of the public school process will induce people to become partners in charting the educational destiny of students.

Through tradition, the operation of a school district is under the control of an elected board of education. This governing body, usually composed of five to seven members, was to provide representation for the people of the district. But since education is also a state function, school boards find themselves in the position of representing the people of an entire state.

District boards of education often have been forced to represent the whole to a far greater degree than their own communities. Every time a school district is enlarged, the board voice of the people is that much thinner. In large urban school districts, one board member may represent as many as seventy thousand students. It is a fact of our political heritage, but not many people understand that local board authority stems from state constitutions and legislative action rather than from the community voters.

If the present trend toward governmental largeness in educational affairs continues, the time will come when students, as the initial clients, will be lost to the sight of those few elected to control the schools.

Paynter Plan Reform One

Organize each elementary school into a Community Education Center, administered and controlled by a council of seven members elected by the voters of the neighborhood served by the elementary school.

By making each elementary school, or area of approximately 600 students, into a Community Education Center, a neighborhood focal point will be established, and local community identity created. Citizen interest in education is at its peak when related to children enrolled in the earliest years of public school instruction. This stems from the young age of the children, their program of fundamental skills, and the feeling that the community has some degree of ownership and control of the school. The greatest inducement to community participation may be found in public concern for improving programs of the elementary schools.

The Founding Fathers, no doubt with intent, omitted any reference to a national system of public schools. Under the Tenth Amendment to the Constitution, the responsibility for education was retained by each of the several independent states, as follows:

The powers not delegated to the United States by the Constitution, nor prohibited by it to the States, are reserved to the States respectively, or to the people (thereof) . . . .

The original and time-honored authority for public education resides in the state governments. Following the leadership of Massachusetts, the other states began to apply various controls on separate local systems. Although far-flung localities have always been granted considerable control over their educational affairs, and public education has developed as a community enterprise, the states have usurped more and more of the traditional local control. Reorganization of school control, with legally elected representatives on a Community Education Council, would restore the local voice.

The concept of this revolutionary reform of public educational control can be illustrated by the schematic below:

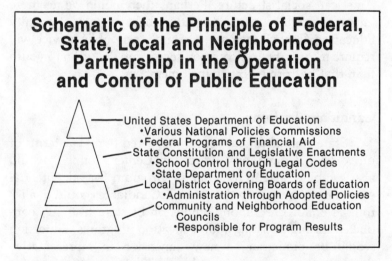

Schematic of the Principle of Federal, State, Local and Neighborhood Partnership in the Operation and Control of Public Education

United States Department of Education
•Various National Policies Commissions
•Federal Programs of Financial Aid
State Constitution and Legislative Enactments
•School Control through Legal Codes
•State Department of Education
Local District Governing Boards of Education
•Administration through Adopted Policies
Community and Neighborhood Education Councils
•Responsible for Program Results

Reorganization of the elementary school, with responsibility for its operation placed in an elected Community Education council, could be accomplished effectively through a popular initiative to amend the state constitution. Or reorganization could be achieved if state legislative action

incorporated into existing codes provisions for the election
and duties of the council. Through either process, the power
and function of council members would be established by
state authority.

Under state constitutional revision or legislative enactment, the legal basis for the election of members to the Community Education Council would be established by the state.
A separate political entity entirely within the boundaries of
existing school districts would result. Such reorganization
would not only broaden public involvement through personal interest, but by actual legislation.

The Community Education Council, elected to represent
the people of the neighborhood, would function under state
authority, with a legally powerful voice. The importance of
such council positions cannot be overstated, for the quality
of elementary education determines the strength of the
American social structure. Perhaps there could be no more
important public office than that held by a Community
Education Council member. Certainly no public service will
require more patience, common sense, and devotion to youth
than that performed by council members.

Candidate Training

State standards, calling for staggered two-year terms of
office on a Community Education Center Council, would
also establish a required training program for all potential
candidate nominees to the council. Candidates could qualify
for the ballot only upon completion of state training, conducted through existing adult education programs. Education
would be pioneering a new dimension in representative
democracy. No longer would candidates unprepared for
public service be elected without some form of training.

The seven-member council would meet monthly. Their
major duty would be to revamp the traditional concept of
representative control of a public institution. Because the

A Glance at Public Opinion

One report from a metropolitan newspaper described a dismal picture of a withdrawn and apathetic public, largely uninformed about the role and activities of local school boards. Nearly two-thirds of the adults polled across the nation were unable to cite a single action taken by their local board of education. An even greater number was unable to name a single board member. A majority did not understand how a school board member was elected.
Major findings of the poll indicated:

1. Easterners and westerners were less likely than southerners and midwesterners to have favorable opinions about their school boards.

2. Twenty-four percent thought school board members and administrators employed were one and the same entity.

3. Twenty-seven percent believed board members served for power, while another twenty percent thought members served to get ahead in politics.

4. Of those adults with children in school, more than two-thirds had not spoken with the teachers, yet nearly one-half had visited the principal or superintendent.

welfare of community elementary education would depend on how intelligently the council performed, all society would be affected.

Through adopted policy, the Community Education Council would be responsible for the administration of the entire elementary program in the Community Education Center. The community's citizens, through elected council representatives, would appoint a director and recommend his dismissal, approve staff selections, determine textbooks and courses of study, and evaluate the results achieved. The Community Education Center would be the true neighborhood school. For the first time, accountability for instructional success would fall under local control.

Mental hygiene, social welfare, reading clinics, extended adult education, and professional counseling services would become an integral part of each Community Education Center. It would be a focal point for community information and services for counseling, from preschool through adulthood. Its total function would reach deeply into the life of the community as a whole.

All major community problems would be addressed first at the Community Education Center—within walking distance for most local citizens. No longer would it be necessary to wander in the maze of state and county buildings to find answers to problems. The use of computer methods and local terminals would make information readily available. If it combined many separate state and federal programs under one administrative complex in every local neighborhood, savings to the American taxpayer could amount to multibillions of dollars annually.

The optimum impact of the Community Education Center would become visible to the public only after a

---

Guidelines for Reformers

1. The establishment of Community Education Centers to replace the elementary schools will require a legal realignment of elected representatives.

2. Reform may depend upon modification of existing education codes or revision of state constitutional provisions.

3. The reform of the elementary schools, carried out through the Community Education Center, should be inaugurated only after an extended program of public information following the development of blueprints for operation.

generation of operation and assessment. But such a plan would ensure our social continuity. The longevity of this nation and democracy could be determined by the success of this revolutionary reform.

13

Three R's Foundation Program

Since Puritan days, Americans have believed that their schools must teach pupils to read, write, and compute basic arithmetic. When that rudimentary learning was coupled with stern attempts to shape the personal, ethical, and moral behavior of our children, often with the aid of a hickory stick, the primary mission of public education was perfectly clear.

The fundamental three R's were the foundation upon which every phase of learning was dependent. Other studies, if carried out at all, were mere adjunct learning experiences. The goal of schools was to provide students with a functional grasp of these three basic tools necessary to enter adult society as productive citizens. Educators, parents, students, and citizens had a known yardstick by which to measure schools, programs, teachers, and student success.

Within the system, the teacher evaluated the success of the materials, facilities, procedures, and methodology. The entire program developed and expanded around the concept of student achievement. For three hundred years, this kind of teaching and learning met broad public approval.

It was obvious that students, well grounded in the three R's, were able to move up to and be absorbed by further education. Students who had mastered the requirements of literacy could soon participate in the work-world of any community. Indeed, this kind of elementary education has a profound effect on the assimilation of widely divergent people living in far-flung areas. It has played a major role in the creation of a unified nation. Citizen groups have been solidified by ensuring to successive generations literacy skills essential to all walks of life.

One of the tragic consequences of population growth in a representative democracy is that in a school district, the voice of the people is decreased because of an ever constant number of elected officials. Control of public education is no exception to this democratic phenomenon. Any fusion of hamlets, villages, and communities into towns, suburbs, and cities removes people further from their elected district board of education members.

This process continues in ever-widening arcs until the elected "voice" falls under the control of selected appointees at state level. Projection of the trend to concentrate populations suggests an eventual national system of public schools. The decision-making "voice" would then emanate from an appointed commission centered in Washington, D.C.

Concentration of power in the hands of distantly based representatives can only dilute the will of local people over the operation of their local schools. If such an eventuality lies in the future, then community control of education must be considered a dead issue. On the other hand, if solutions to the general indictments hurled at the system can be found at the local level, school control can revert to the people most directly affected.

The principle of local control is applicable to every element of representative government. Both school and government functions may be accomplished best under an "umbrella" of community, district, state and national partnership. This is the key to reform of the public schools. A "Foundation Program"—compulsory instruction in the fundamental skills—to be offered in each Community Education Center, will provide a radically new concept of school accountability, evaluted by the public at the neighborhood level.

Progressive and modern education has been forced upon the schools through decisions made by leaders often farthest removed from the local scene. Each time the curriculum has been expanded, school objectives become more comprehensive, vague, and difficult to measure. The main thrust of modern intellectual opinion has been to undermine acceptable school standards. It has denigrated objectives. The absence of objectives creates a void in any valid means of evaluation. Today, instructional measurement is just not possible; no one is apparently accountable to anyone!

The new methods of teaching and revised materials often diminish public understanding and support of programs. Educational change, largely generated, planned, and administered at the state level, rarely meets public approval. People know no valid means exists today by which the community can evalute school achievement. Consequently, every departure from the traditional three R's as the schools' main purpose fosters a breakdown in understanding between educators and the public.

Sometime after 1925, the idea of a restricted elementary course of studies was pushed aside in favor of a new philosophy mandated by state intervention in the curriculum. Little by little, new courses were legislated into the curriculum and methods revised until the basic purpose of the public schools became all-inclusive. No longer did the teacher instruct; he or she became a passive advisor or a kind of "resource friend" to the student.

The chief purpose of school became social achievement rather than intellectual achievement. Instead of teaching children to master optimum skills within their individual ranges of different abilities, schools welcomed the dilution of the academic program. Educators substituted an array of curriculum attempts to help underprivileged and emotionally disturbed students adjust to life. The teaching function was reduced to the development of social attitudes rather than the instillation of literacy. The door was open for schools to teach everything in which achievement was most difficult to measure.

Every modern modification of the central mission of the schools adds required subjects into the elementary course of study. Each curricular revision depletes effort once expended on the teaching of basic skills. Revision does not lend itself to objective measurement, and goals are impossible to define clearly enough for public acceptance. Innovation has created instruction programs without content, to say nothing of objectives. The progressive movement, carried out by state intervention and federal encouragement, has created a curriculum in which the three R's have all been overlooked.

Definitions of a course of study are now all-inclusive. Every pupil experience and extracurricular activity directed by the school has become a part of the total learning process. This curriculum expansion has grown in direct proportion to the growth of state and national influence over schools. Subjects have become more numerous in an attempt "to meet the needs of a more complex society." The schools now challenge the home as the focal point for all instructional responsibility. The elementary process has shortchanged millions of youngsters by placing curricular emphasis on mere instructional frills. Today, recess often receives more attention than the fundamental three R's. But the need for student mastery of the three R's has never changed one iota.

The cycle of progressive innovation, fads, and curriculum alternatives has run its tragic course. Public and educator are stalemated. The former equates student achievement with literacy skills needed in everyday life; the latter intends to be held accountable for nonmeasurable activities. The result is an impasse built of "seat time," boredom, and social promotion, with little emphasis on performance-based progress. Countless numbers of functional illiterates pour yearly from our school system. One research study indicates that the nation today is confronted with more than 23 million people who cannot read or write at the sixth grade level.

Paynter Plan Reform Two

Establish a Foundation Program of compulsory instruction in the fundamental three R's, required of all children enrolled in every Community Center, each under the direction of seven-member Community Education Councils.

Public schools have been the victims of a decade without respect, which has undermined acceptable curricular offerings and standards. People themselves have ushered in this age of permissiveness. Naturally, public schools are affected. But, no matter the fault, until people become accountable for their actions, no correction can come about. Successful change must be built around a new breed of parent, administrator, teacher, and student.

Basic education, through the Foundation Program, is defined as the teaching of the three R's to the great mass of children. Public schools are for the largest number of youth possible. And universal, free, and compulsory education in the United States includes in that great mass of youth all students as opposed to a system for the privileged few.

Any program of fundamental education must achieve its purpose without limitation or discrimination. And success must be measurable by a public satisfied with valid and understandable results. The very purpose of the Foundation Program, to be offered in every Community Education Center, is to achieve that goal. Anything less means that the school has failed in its major purpose.

The single objective of the Foundation Program is to provide the tools of literacy for every student. Elementary instruction must be directed to the teaching of the three R's, the very means whereby students profit from all further educational experiences.

A California Department of Education report released in May of 1980 indicated that more than thirty percent of the 1980-81 high school seniors would miss graduation because they could not, in all probability, pass state-mandated, minimum competency tests in the three R's. Almost half the school districts surveyed reported that up to thirty percent of the students failed the tests. Nineteen percent of the districts said that up to forty percent had failed while thirty-one percent stated that *more than* forty percent had failed. To avoid such statistics, the first six years of schooling must be based squarely upon these three basics—a goal that the system has pushed aside during the past fifty years, even though it is the goal demanded by the society for which the schools exist.

Dedication to Basics

During the past decade, the number one criticism of public schools, according to dozens of opinion polls, has been their inability to maintain acceptable standards of obedience to rules and respect for authority. People also questioned the schools' ability to control the essentials of mental discipline. People want boys and girls to learn the skills needed in the modern society. People believe that the collapse of discipline has created a system of too much schooling providing too little education.

Any differentiation between schooling and education creates emotional outbursts. Legislative mandates asking evaluations for accountability run head-on into educational union-type associations. Yet, the movement toward reform exerts increasing pressure on the entire system.

The public knows that all students must master the basic skills embodied in the three R's yet it does not realize that success depends upon instruction measured by performance standards which evaluate student achievement and govern progress through the various levels of the system. It is predictable that the Foundation Program will run afoul of teacher organizations which, in some cases, flatly reject the notion of performance accountability.

The Foundation Program of elementary instruction offered in each Community Education Center will provide the core of the entire curriculum. The single goal of each teacher will be to teach the fundamentals of literacy. Without exception, all staff members in the Foundation Program must be trained specialists in the teaching of reading, writing, and arithmetic. Few teachers beyond the third grade are prepared to teach reading, yet students are passed on to them without reading skills. The primary purpose of compulsory elementary school years is to guarantee student achievement of demonstrable skills at the sixth grade level. Measurable results form the only criteria by which school, staff, student, and parental success may be determined by the community.

The curriculum of each Community Education Center, no matter the extent of course titles or subject matter content, must be taught in direct relationship to reading, writing, and arithmetic. The Foundation Program must not be permitted to deviate from ensuring student mastery of these essentials. This reform places the primary responsibility on the system to teach students to become literate. The student and his or her parents, however, become accountable to the community for learning the fundamentals of literacy.

The Most Essential R

Reading ability, more than anything else in the elementary curriculum, makes possible the skills that permit everyone to educate himself or herself. The major function of the Foundation Program is to teach children to read. The educational process begins with ingrained student desire to read, for all children want to read. But the task of the teacher is to build the desire until it becomes infused in students as a socioeconomic necessity.

Perhaps the methodology will remain secondary in nature; certainly the instructional materials matter even less. But reading is the one skill upon which literacy is founded. Writing, the ability to do arithmetic, understanding of history, geography, and science—all depend upon reading achievement. In no other area does education's social accountability play such a vital role in the lives of people who are the next generation. The reading instruction must affect the entire curriculum of the Foundation Program.

The results of fifty years of liberalized education have now reached a political turning point. In the name of the people, lawmakers are now trying to force teachers to teach those subjects that can be measured. Everyone wants the school system to achieve its mission in the training of youngsters in the fundamental skills of literacy.

Public criticism also equates deteriorating discipline and illiteracy in school age youth with crime and violence. How can student interest in a school program remain high when the materials and methods cannot be understood? Aimless drifting through the schools is one result. Student violence has surely been one unhappy signal that reform is long overdue.

Elementary instruction offered in the Foundation Program can become a reality only through a drastic change in educational philosophy. The fundamental curriculum asks what are the purposes, the content, and the means of measurement; it's not so much concerned with the methods of instruction. It is not indifferent to social, ethical, and vocational career development of students. But public education can be justified only when all students master the fundamentals of literacy.

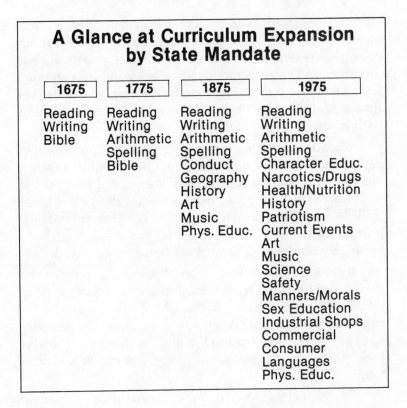

A Glance at Curriculum Expansion by State Mandate

1675	1775	1875	1975
Reading	Reading	Reading	Reading
Writing	Writing	Writing	Writing
Bible	Arithmetic	Arithmetic	Arithmetic
	Spelling	Spelling	Spelling
	Bible	Conduct	Character Educ.
		Geography	Narcotics/Drugs
		History	Health/Nutrition
		Art	History
		Music	Patriotism
		Phys. Educ.	Current Events
			Art
			Music
			Science
			Safety
			Manners/Morals
			Sex Education
			Industrial Shops
			Commercial
			Consumer
			Languages
			Phys. Educ.

Standards Must Be Set

The completion of the third grade usually ends the introductory phase of schooling. Perhaps this is because visible extremes in academic achievement can now be observed. It is not uncommon for any ordinary group of fourth grade students to represent a span of several years in ability, even though they may all be the same age chronologically.

Although not necessarily a mid-point in the compulsory school years, most nine-year-old students have gone through a complete orientation of the learning process. In one sense, they have been weaned from the home. Most of them are ready to enter the intermediate grades.

The natural break in the school experience demands formulation of additional objectives. Intermediate teachers begin the specialized remedial instruction to correct student deficiencies. Consequently, one checkpoint to determine school accomplishment falls naturally at the third grade. The final measurement of student progress will culminate at the sixth grade.

The goal to teach students to master the basic three R's never wavers in the Community Education Center. Teachers must teach and students must learn literacy skills; otherwise, both have failed. Student progress toward this goal must be evident; anything less than measurable achievement relegates learning to the acquisition of just so much common "horse sense," which does not answer modern social demands.

If the goal of the Foundation Program is to teach students to master the three R's, then specific standards must be established to ascertain progress. At the conclusion of the compulsory attendance years, students must be achieving sixth grade results in reading, writing, and arithmetic before they can continue with voluntary programs of public instruction.

Grades on traditional report cards and promotion to the next grade have proved unreliable indicators of either school or student success. Whatever the teacher has taught remains hidden unless tangible evidence measures progress. Whatever the child may have learned also remains hidden unless literacy permits measurement of the results.

Demonstrable evidence of student achievement has been generally misunderstood. Valid measurement, illusive in nature, is represented by wide variations in statistical results. Overall data has proved meaningless. In fact, student achievement is probably the most poorly measured activity by any public institution. It is doubtful that school funds will continue to be appropriated unless meaningful results from standardized tests can be provided. Legislators are bound to require validated success of school programs. One public opinion poll indicates that nearly two-thirds of those questioned agree that standardized test data is essential to any evaluation of educational accomplishments.

Success of the Foundation Program will be subject to community approval at every step of the compulsory elementary process. Approval will be based on periodic measurement by criterion—referenced tests administered to large samples of third and sixth grade students to document goals achievement. Twin checkpoints of progress in the basic three R's at the third and sixth grade levels can serve three other purposes:

1. Standardized test data could provide the basis for "in-house" evaluation of program, system, and student success, from which would come the development of a performance index to determine possible modification.

2. Standardized test data could form the basis for statewide allocation of school funds for program improvement to place compulsory education on a financial index for public scrutiny.

3. Standardized test data could form the basis for national assessment of student achievement in the fundamental three R's on which a school, district, state, and national performance index would be based.

Local Control of Staff

Perhaps the most significant impact of the Foundation Program will be community control over the preparation required of educators in each Community Education Center. Local determination of instruction standards will rest on public review of the qualifications and special attributes of faculty members. Each person on the staff will have a personal dossier available for inspection by all parents.

The record of professional training for school educators is placed on the line; teacher background is open to community judgment through parental assessment. The professional judgment of the personnel director is also placed on open view, for he is responsible for the employment of the staff members.

The dossier for every staff member, no matter the grade level, subject, or assignment, will include a picture, record of college training for major or specialization, degree received, credentials held, date of course work, and honors or awards. The dossier will present a profile from which parents may determine competency. For the first time in the history of public education, a certificated profile of their instructors will be available to parents before their children enter school.

The dossier also acts as a motivation for teachers. The instructor with one degree, little specialization, no particular recognition or recent training may be subjected to professional embarrassment and set out to improve his skills. The results would upgrade both the professional competence of staff and the overall pride in the profession of teaching.

The process of staff selection is continued throughout the years of compulsory education in the Foundation Program. Personal student accountability for elementary achievement will culminate only when the student enters into voluntary educational programs or leaves school for some kind of employment. But the greatest value of this community control comes through the building of confidence of staff in the eyes of the public. Educators, selected and retained at the will of the community, would be trusted to guarantee that all boys and girls would master the basic skills of literacy.

In addition to checkpoints at the third and sixth grades to measure student achievement and staff accomplishment, "in house" assessment of pupil progress will be continuous. Systematic monitoring of student performance is an integral part of each staff member's professional responsibility. But certificated employees cannot be held accountable without application of sound administrative evaluation procedures. These must take the highest priority in the duties of the Community Education Center director. Staff appraisal as now practiced is conducted mostly as a required afterthought to the everyday administrative functions.

Sensational stories in the media blame educational deterioration for lack of discipline, loss of morality, and the absence of standards. Polls indicate, too, that people believe schools have de-emphasized or removed difficult studies from the curriculum because boys and girls cannot learn them. Worse yet, many people believe student ability to read and write has all but disappeared. Even college officials have climbed on this bandwagon to condemn teaching and learning performance. The ironic outcome has been professional silence or, at least, inadequate response from the educators.

Educators seek to retain the authority to determine the standards by which student progress may be measured. But they refuse to undergo their own professional evaluation equated with student performance. This inconsistency will be resolved only when funding for public education becomes dependent upon the degree of student success in demonstrable test results.

Testing the Tests

When school income is directly related to testing performance data, the data will become the all-important basis for monitoring student progress.

If allocation of school funds is to be based on student achievement as determined by test results, then the teaching-learning process must be judged by relevant test data. If the instrument is valid for state funding, it must be accurate enough for the staff to teach the test items.

This concept opens the door to new methodology. Teachers will develop teaching strategies to meet the test. The new procedure is no different than most situations in actual adult life. The driver's test for an automobile operator's license contains no item not included in the instructional manual. Few housewives ever bake a cake without the recipe right in front of them. If teaching the test items fails to produce acceptable student achievement, perhaps the test should be revised . . . or the methods . . . or the materials . . . or the very system itself.

If the single most important goal of all elementary instruction is to ensure that boys and girls master the fundamental skills at the sixth grade level, then all testing should concentrate on a valid way to appraise student performance. The criterion must become the focal point around which instruction revolves. That is why the Foundation Program is geared strictly to providing documentary evidence of pupil progress in the literacy skills. There is no other valid reason for administering a test battery to students. When the goal determines the purpose of elementary instruction in the Community Education Center, the choice of methods and materials utilized by the teacher to meet the goal are of little importance—so long as productive results can be documented.

When the public holds schools responsible for student success as the basis of state allocation of funds, then the system will become truly accountable to the community it serves. Effective educational reform means that if students fail to progress, the entire process must be examined and changed to meet the goal.

One of the most significant components of all reform may be introduced with a built-in, staff-oriented safeguard. Promotion, grade levels, and report cards make no difference; they will have no bearing on student achievement in the Foundation Program. Instead, every teacher will be required to confirm student progress at the completion of semester or yearly intervals by signed personal verification of each student's achievement. This means the teacher's professional reputation is at stake. So, too, will be the credibility of the administration. All stand accountable to the community.

When the students, with their signed certificates of achievement, enter the next grade of elementary experience in the Foundation Program, they will be given an approved pretest to verify performance levels. If ten percent of the students from any specific teacher fail to confirm the signed performance level for two successive years, the salary of that teacher will be reduced. Also, when ten percent of the staff members have issued certificates of achievement unable to be verified by successful completion of the subsequent pretest, the administration and all supporting nonteaching personnel face identical reduction in salaries. This may sound harsh, but effective control over rote "seat time" and automatic promotion regardless of achievement is essential.

Under the Foundation Program, the contemporary report card system may well be abolished in the Community Education Center. The usual rating procedures will be eliminated by an administrative regulation requiring the teachers to report student progress in a manner determined with each individual parent. This practice will accomplish three very important functions:

1. It will force teachers to develop closer ties with parents to create a unique bond between school and home.

2. It will terminate the continual haggle over report card types and values of teacher marks.

3. It will mandate parental choice of an acceptable reporting system.

Parental selection of the appropriate grading system is the initial step in building productive, community-school relationships. Perhaps, in this manner, the Community Education Center will persuade society to consider education more seriously than ever before. Certainly, the schools can serve the community only when citizens participate actively in their evaluation. If this could be accomplished, the problem of public relations would be reduced to a minimum.

Third, Sixth Grade Checkouts

In addition to teacher reports to parents, the Community Education Center will place special emphasis on reporting the results of pupil achievement at the third and sixth grade check-points. Interpretation of standardized test data requires professional expertise now unknown in public education. But, on the staff of each Community Education Center will be a Parent Reporting Specialist whose function will be to assemble into a profile the student's record of achievement, illness and absence reports, and all information related to other learning disabilities. The Specialist will report the findings to the parents of every third and sixth grade student, explaining the data so that parents understand the exact ability of their childen in reading, writing, and arithmetic. It is extremely difficult for both parent and teacher to be totally objective when discussing student progress.

This objective staff member must possess unique credentials: professional skills, patience, accuracy, honesty, and integrity. Above all, the specialist is employed to provide professional help to the teachers. He or she will maintain a quiet office where parents may discuss the student's achievement record. The specialist will explain what the staff has done for the student up to the third grade level, what the performance record indicates, and what the plans involve for the following three years.

The process will be repeated at the sixth grade and at this point professional counseling services will originate. At this time the record and the rapport established between home and school by the specialist will become crucial. This is the completion of compulsory education. This is the moment for parental and student decision affecting the future endeavors of the youngster.

One of the keys to the success of the Paynter Plan is that the school structure must be designed to separate compulsory from voluntary public education. The Foundation Program will provide elementary instruction on a required basis only through the sixth grade. The experiences offered at the Community Education Center conclude the state's responsibility to ensure public literacy. Including two years of preschool and kindergarten training, a total of eight years of instruction is provided under compulsory attendance laws and required literacy achievement levels.

14

Taking It to the Teachers

The traditional evaluation process in the public schools has always been carried out by a downward flow of authority, from the board of education to the superintendent to the directors to the principals to the teachers, and finally to the students. Its effectiveness has always been dependent upon two factors.

Each administrator must be competent in those areas that he or she is expected to measure and must have the time to conduct proper evaluation of staff members. Even with these factors, evaluation may not be true. Administrative efforts to please a superior in the hierarchy may create totally incorrect evaluation.

One of the ironic developments in public education during the last decade has been the spiraling increase in complex administrative duties unrelated to improvement of actual classroom instruction. Today's school manager has become the educational leader. Most modern day principals are business-oriented facilitators. They have little time for supervising study programs.

Often evaluation is not much more than a nod of the head or a cursory completion of a checklist on teacher personality, grooming, and punctuality. Functional evaluation is nearly unknown in today's public schools.

As the authority for the evaluation process flows downward, it is counterbalanced by an informal appraisal upward. The student first declares the teacher did not provide adequate instruction; the teacher then charges the principal refused to provide support or materials. The principal blames the district regulations or the director, who then challenges the superintendent with setting improper financial priorities. The finger is finally pointed at the board of education, which often hides behind state laws enacted under pressure from people demanding change. Accusations stem from a lack of individual success.

In the Paynter Plan, the responsibility for quality instruction is focused directly on the classroom teacher. Evaluations should begin with the teacher. They would end with the board of education.

Only through drastic reform of educational assessment practices will administrators relinquish certain traditional responsibilties downward, but the burden of performance must be placed on those who are employed to produce specific accomplishments. The classroom teacher must be granted full authority to carry out the instructional program, with the single goal being student achievement at a stipulated and acceptable level of performance. This means the Foundation Program of elementary instruction must be measured on student progress toward the mastery of the three R's at the sixth grade performance level.

Paynter Plan Reform Three

Delegate full authority to each Community Education Center classroom teacher and hold each responsible for the success of pupil achievement, resulting

in control of all expenditure of funds designated for
pupil instruction.

So long as the laws of this country prohibit thirteen to sixteen-year-old youth from entering the labor market, the taxpayer will continue to believe in compulsory attendance. The goal is to keep youngsters off the street and within the custodial institution. But the longer boys and girls are required to remain in school, the lower acceptable standards become. Reform will improve the quality of public education while reducing the compulsory attendance factor.

Whenever community support backs the effort to require schools to prove measurable achievement, the effort is successful. Communities that hold educators and students responsible demand a new attitude on the part of both. An instruction program designed to be successful always begins with the hypothesis that students *can* learn, no matter what the social and environmental factors are surrounding them.

The questions then become administrative: how much, how fast, and at what cost. Underlying each concern is the question of personal motivation to encourage new directions for instructional improvement in the Foundation Program. Valid reform begins when those charged with accountability are delegated the authority to carry out the process providing measurable proof of results.

Fiscal responsibility is in direct relationship to accountability for all elements in the school operation, for the Community Education Council is obligated to inform the public of the results of performance assessment. True reform opens the way for an evaluation index on a person-to-person basis. The school performance is reduced to a measurement of results by individuals in control of all factors necessary to guarantee student achievement. With this control in the hands of classroom teachers, they are subject to individual accountability for personal performance. "Buck passing" is eliminated.

Teacher Calls the Budget Tune

The overall education budget is determined by state and local funds. Costs for central administration, transportation, maintenance, and other static operations are clear. The remainder of the budget delineates instructional costs. The proportionate share becomes the operational income for each Community Education Center. These budgeted funds become available to each teacher for draw purposes, to carry out the instruction program.

Each teacher is granted the funding for specific classroom instruction on a per student ratio. If the budget allocates $2,000 per pupil, then a teacher with thirty-two students would control an expenditure of $64,000 for a particular classroom program. If there were twenty-five students, the teacher controlled budget would be $50,000 for that classroom program. No longer would state funding be considered a complex operation. Nor would the state financing of public schools need to deviate from the *Serrano Case*, which requires statewide equity of funding for equal education opportunities.

The mechanics of school expenditures would be reduced to a one-teacher operation, in which each would become accountable for the results achieved by students enrolled in his or her specific classroom.

The primary function of the director of the center would be to provide staff support services as a facilitator. His or her evaluation would come from the assessment of the supporting role performed.

It is quite possible administrative costs could be reduced in keeping with the modified duties assigned.

A base salary for the teaching staff would be formulated and adopted by the district board of education. Teachers would make individual determinations of expenditures necessary for their classrooms. Each teacher makes the decision of *how* the money will be spent. Each teacher determines the selection and purchase of all necessary curriculum supplies, resource materials, and specialized professional services.

But expenditures for supplies and services would reduce funds available for the teacher salary above the base schedule. Rather than salary or budget negotiating being the prime consideration of the administration, it will be evaluation of program effectiveness and personnel performance.

If paraprofessional classroom aides, substitutes, or refresher college courses are necessary to help overcome learning handicaps, the fees will come out of the teacher controlled budget. Teacher salary, above the adopted base schedule, would be determined by the teacher. Each teacher would make the decision how to spend budget instructional funds.

This reform will change the traditionally accepted components of teacher power. No longer will organization, unity, and commitment be collective in nature. Political clout in the state legislatures and congressional halls will be created by the image of successful educators who control the curriculum, materials, textbooks, specialized resources, class size, and salaries.

With teacher control of expenditures for classroom instruction comes a professional obligation to guarantee student achievement in the fundamental three R's. The teacher is held accountable to the Community Education Council for results.

If teachers seek to improve their own skills, they make the decision to spend the money out of their classroom budget. All money must be used to guarantee student success. The teaching staff of the Community Education Center will require a professional training background different from present college training.

Acceptance of a contract signifies a professional commitment by the teacher to accomplish the educational task within allocated instructional funds. At long last, teacher evaluation would be equated with actual student performance

and expenditure of school monies. A valid personnel performance index would be created.

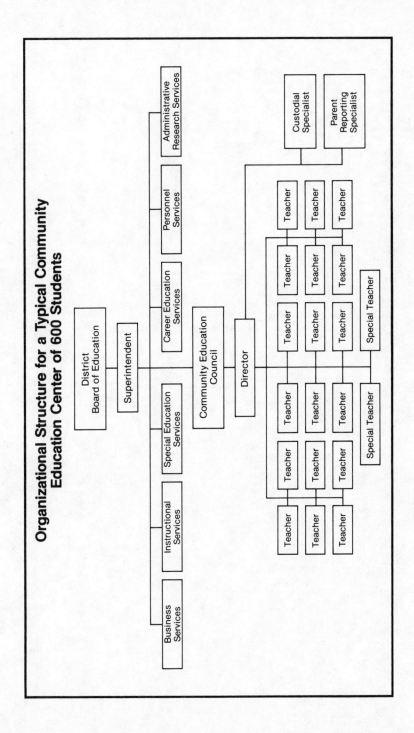

Organizational Structure for a Typical Community Education Center of 600 Students

15

The World After the Sixth Grade

Reform of the elementary school process does not refute the concept of compulsory education. All youth must be required to master the skills of literacy. The Foundation Program offered in every Community Education Center will provide such elementary instruction to all boys and girls on a compulsory basis through the sixth grade.

All youth will receive two years of preschool experience, known as Early Childhood Education and Kindergarten, to be followed by six years of instruction in the literacy skills.

Eight years of public school instruction will be provided under compulsory laws and mandated achievement testing to meet required proficiency standards. Only then will the doors of publicly financed secondary instruction, comprising six years of voluntary career development, be open to those students who have mastered the skills of literacy. The first two years of college training will offer a student "career refinement" opportunities, be they academic or for immediate vocational transition into the adult society. Although voluntary in nature, these two years of college must be completed successfully before the student can enter the extensive research required by upper level and graduate school programs.

Paynter Plan Reform Four

Compulsory attendance regulations will cease at the conclusion of the sixth grade, after which professional counseling services will aid each individual family to determine the appropriateness of further voluntary programs of education.

Publicly financed secondary instruction will be available only to those students with sixth grade competency in the fundamental three R's. This ensures that students who continue in the voluntary programs will be able to profit from state financed instruction at the secondary level.

At the conclusion of the Foundation Program, parents and student, aided by professional counseling services, will determine the student's future direction. The custodial obligation has ceased at the end of the sixth grade. By the age of thirteen years, students who have not yet shown desire for formal instruction are not likely to profit from further compulsory educational experiences.

Out with Fads

Educational reform must root out the entrenched philosophy: try any fad once.

Common Learnings, the Core Curriculum, flexible scheduling, technical, vocational, and career education in the course of studies are examples. Special aid for the gifted or unmotivated students affect less than five percent of enrolled students. Few of these experiments have ever altered the basic institution. None offers a strong plan for survival of our system of public education.

A Glance at the Reform of Public Education

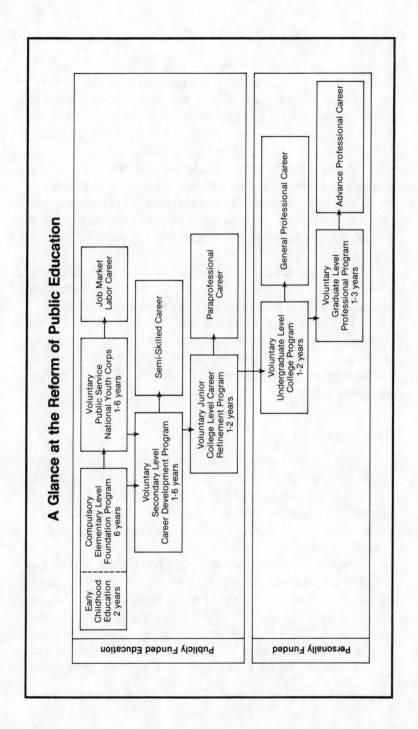

The concept that secondary education should begin at age thirteen, after six years of instruction in the fundamental three R's, is historically well founded. Nearly every European nation follows the practice. After fifty years of American experimentation with eight years of elementary instruction, few consider the extended years essential.

The eight grade pattern of elementary instruction can be traced to Horace Mann's influence during the mid-point of the last century. Borrowed from Germany, the intention of a seventh and eighth grade was to offer the great mass of people all the public education necessary for them to become literate.

Until the 1920s, many people believed elementary instruction ended at the sixth grade. In fact, Salt Lake City refused to include the 8th grade in its elementary system until after World War II. Neither the college-bound nor the dropout youth was affected adversely. Evidence is mounting once again that the recommendations of the 1893 *National Committee of Ten* and the 1905 *National Council of Five* were correct.

The Thirteen-Year-Old Is Ready

Both reports declared that eight years of compulsory attendance was too long for elementary instruction; both implied that thirteen-year-old boys and girls were to be considered as ready for a new kind of voluntary educational experience. Both reports were based on the concept of individual choice.

The purpose of the seventh and eighth grades has become less to educate boys and girls than to counsel, orient, or guide them to make the proper vocational choice. The notion that public education is open to all is deeply ingrained in our culture. No one would abolish this educational heritage. But in reality, the world looks upon the high school as providing a meaningless extension of elementary instruction.

The great tragedy is that our basic system tries to push fifty percent of the students into an academic program. Students are forced to miss valid career development instruction. Subsequently, "on-the-job" training becomes the norm.

Even in the most revolutionary system, the educational needs of all youth will not be met within the compulsory attendance years. For some, additional secondary career development schooling is doubtful or refused. A choice must be open to them and their parents, available through publicly financed programs.

When a thirteen-year-old youngster helps make his first important decision, when he elects to leave home, when he finds his first job, or when he enjoys several hours of lightly supervised leisure time, he will be more likely to appreciate his own personal educational needs. Many learning opportunities are available to boys and girls after completion of the compulsory six grades. The most valuable lesson educators may learn is that all youths continue to grow in some direction, no matter what their achievement records in the public schools show.

Youth Corps One Answer

The establishment of a federally funded National Youth Corps, patterned after the Civilian Conservation Corps of the 1930s and the Job Corps Conservation Corps of the 1960s, could provide practical, postelementary instruction for those students who choose to leave school after the compulsory years. The corps could be joined for from one to six years.

Some unusual facts about changes in family life can be linked to radical differences in family working habits. In 1974, more than half of all mothers with school-aged children worked full-time. Seventy-five years ago, single parent families with children were headed by some relative other than the mother. Just as family patterns have changed, the accepted morality of young adults has modified home life. In

1945, about one of every twenty-five women gave birth to an illegitimate child. This ratio has increased to one of eight.

Today, more and more children are reared in homes representing little more than a dormitory-type shell. Such youngsters have no parental care; they grow up under the questionable guidance of baby sitters. Millions of children spend more time in outright idleness than under parental or school training. These circumstances provide for a "dropout" syndrome in the contemporary setting.

> A major part of the blame for today's high dropout rate is being placed on the nation's rising divorce rate and the resulting breakup of families. Myra Sampson, principal of Chicago's Community Christian Alternative Academy, puts it this way: "One of the biggest causes goes back to the family. The family today is not what it was years back." Dropouts typically are from broken homes, she adds, where baby-sitting and financial needs conflict with the children's going to school.
>
> Dropouts come from every economic and social stratum, but there is a higher proportion among the poor and minorities. The rate among blacks is about twice that among white youngsters—49.6 dropouts for every 100 black graduates, compared with 23.3 per 100 white graduates, according to the Bureau of Labor Statistics.[1]

Youngsters who have joined the ranks of the dropouts might find a "home" in a National Youth Corps. Here a teenager would be subject to learning and work, both influential in the development of attitudes toward life. Perhaps here may be found the primary ingredient necessary for successful education. Real learning comes to the teenager who participates in the choice of his or her own direction.

Membership in the corps could preserve youthful morale and raise adult expectations. Educational experiences, in the

---

[1]Education, "What's Being Done About Dropouts?" Reprinted from *U.S. News & World Report*, June 2, 1980, p. 64. "Copyright 1980 *U.S. News & World Report*, Inc."

form of conservation work combined with related instruction, would be the total function. A youth could learn a skill, improve tools of literacy, and accomplish socially useful tasks. A member would receive room, board, clothing, and limited spending money. A youngster would work while earning his or her learning.

This particular generation has the same need for public work that youth can perform as it had in the 1930s. No longer would those who are most ill prepared for society be left in idleness. The cost of a National Youth Corps would be far less than the cost of increased police forces to curb teenage violence and crime rate. The lowering of compulsory attendance laws to the sixth grade would open up freedom of parental-child choice of varied alternatives.

In the last thirty years, young adults went back to school by the millions. They returned to programs and courses of their own choosing after a voluntary dropping out, after military service, after finding and losing the first job, or after some personal nonschool experience. Competency and proficiency gained from a National Youth Corps, coupled with education by choice, would bring a new type of public evaluation to the public school system.

Individual desire to learn comes from within a person. Public education cannot ensure student achievement any more than a theological seminary can produce doctrinal faith. Away from the formal structure of the school process, students have been known to win on their own initiative gold medals and Eagle Scout rank, to spend months studying wildlife, soil and water conservation, forestry and geology. Many a youth who might become highly proficient in such subjects while a member of the National Youth Corps might have barely achieved minimum standards in compulsory classes at the public schools.

The task of public education, including a National Youth Corps, is to create interest, provide opportunities, and offer facilities to those students who seek to learn.

16

Education
As You Like It

Public education's goal must be to make possible a productive and worthwhile life for every citizen. At no point is education ever considered as completed. Learning is continuous throughout a person's lifetime. Educational opportunities must be made available to all who wish them, or society can expect only further decadence. Neither the age nor scholarship level of the learner should alter the basic function of the schools. Statistics indicate that too many "uneducated" adults return to the classroom. This shows a drastic need to revamp the system.

More than one state has opened the door to an alternative means for pupils to leave school. Its law states that a high school proficiency examination may be administered to any interested sixteen or seventeen-year-old student. Upon successful completion of the test with an acceptable score, the student will be awarded a "Certificate of Proficiency" by the state board of education. This preempts local school district jurisdiction and makes an "end-run" around the compulsory attendance laws upon which secondary school programs are now so dependent. It moves school control even further from the community.

This law is the initial attempt to modify the school structure. One ironic factor may be revealed from the statistical results. The number of students who attempt the examination may indicate a widespread dislike for the schools. The number of students who pass the examination and receive the state certificate will provide an unusual yardstick to measure the educational success of each school district.

The number of passing students who then withdraw from school, but do not seek to continue their learning in college or trade school, will most likely join the ranks of those who try for some form of public welfare. The most devastating statistic may be the number of students who fail the examination. They will have to remain in school and may spend those semesters flaunting the learning process by willful disobedience, violence, and rebellion.

Efforts to reform public education require more than a reduction of the compulsory age for school attendance. By itself, this action would create a point of time beyond which the dropout would become legal. Without a program for those youngsters who leave the classrooms, millions would be destined to enter a two or three year period of idleness. Too young to meet the existing labor laws, which prohibit them from entering the work market, and too disinterested in further school learning, such boys and girls would be free to run the streets.

Volunteer to Learn

The Paynter Plan for reform calls for an extension of voluntary learning programs. Its recommendation of compulsory attendance laws only through the sixth grade is based upon the theory that when students possess the basic skills of the three R's, they are prepared to profit from all further programs of public financed education which they may then select on a voluntary basis. Students who fail to reach a sixth grade ability to read, write, and compute mathematics require massive remedial programs throughout the entire learning process—a vast waste of public funds.

Elementary education under the Community Education Center must spill over into the secondary phase. High school programs must present a revitalized curriculum for acceptable career development, open to voluntary enrollment.

When students meet the standards of the Foundation Program, public assessment of the Community Education Center will be completed. The public cannot claim that schools are unsuccessful. Test scores from the third and sixth grade levels will be explained to each parent, the composite results made public. Local satisfaction with statewide measurable standards should underwrite an upswing in national educational programs. The federal principle of school partnership through community, district, state, and national participation would flourish to support the interests of all.

If students cannot demonstrate competency in the three R's, the system is, in fact, held responsible. Teachers, counselors, resource specialists, and administrators will be forced to explain the failure. Every parent will have a direct voice in the assessment of the schools. The process of compiling data to isolate reasons for failure will open the way to corrective measures. For the first time in public education, many avenues of statistical evidence may be used by all staff members to upgrade the system. This is the very foundation upon which true educational professionalism rests.

The Taxpayer's Burden

The American taxpayer contributed nearly $110 billion during 1975 to educate youth in this nation's public schools. This figure represents an annual investment of just over $500 per capita. When these figures are adjusted to apply only to actual wage earners, public education requires a yearly expenditure of nearly $1,500 per taxpaying citizen. Considering the extent of this burden on the American worker, it is no wonder that people seek to assess the school situation in the light of dollar cost.

This nation enjoys the highest standard of living in the world. Yet, the records reveal an astonishing number of students who despise all forms of learning. It has been estimated that, at any given time, 2.4 million school-age youths are not in school, according to the latest Census Bureau figures. A look at school-dropout rates cited below is again illuminating—and disturbing.

Where Many Quit High School

One method to determine high-school-dropout rates is to compare the number of graduates with the ninth-grade enrollment four years earlier. Here's how 15 large cities compare, based on latest enrollment figures—

	Percent Not Graduating
Chicago	52%
St. Louis	52%
Detroit	51%
New York	49%
Baltimore	45%
Cleveland	40%
Philadelphia	40%
Washington, D.C.	40%
Memphis	39%
Milwaukee	34%
Dallas	33%
Houston	33%
Phoenix	31%
Los Angeles	30%
San Diego	29%

Note: Dropout rates in some cities may be exaggerated because of shrinking school-age populations.

USN&WR table—Basic date: U.S. Dept. of Education

Most of the dropouts are headed for the lowest rung in the social ladder, where they will stay. Of those who remain enrolled in the schools, crime, alcohol, and drugs have become a major influence on the lives of many secondary students. College entrance scores have taken a downward plunge.

Through school reform requiring demonstrable proficiency in the three R's, deficient students would not be able to enter postelementary *voluntary* programs funded at public expense. No matter the option selected, the future direction of every youth, beginning at grade seven, will be determined by personal interest, aptitude, and motivation. All course and attendance requirements vanish; new learning experience is through self-directed programs of career related instruction.

Paynter Plan Reform Five

Abolish the distribution of tax funds as district income based on pupil attendance. Institute a legal system of financing voluntary postelementary education through the use of Student Learning Certificates. These would be available to all youth upon completion of the sixth grade, and may be cashed at any time during a subsequent thirteen-year period, at individual discretion, in payment for enrollment at any approved institution.

The greatest change of this reform, besides its alteration of the financial base for all postelementary education, will be the student's personal determination of the programs desired, the location of schools or institutions where particular types of instruction are found, and the open competition between schools for students. At an end will be the temptation for parental dishonesty, covering absenteeism through false excuses, and the need for district padding of attendance figures, requiring time-consuming and expensive truancy activities. Also ended will be the financial penalties now applied against school districts when student absentee rates soar.

The importance of the Student Learning Certificate for educational financing will become evident in the improvement of courses, methods, and school administration. It will make no difference what kind of school is involved in competition for student enrollment, although one that offers second-rate programs will stand to lose its financial support when students enroll elsewhere. For the student now becomes the primary client. The entire educational operation becomes a student-centered operation.

The American system of free, universal, and compulsory education provides more formal schooling than many students desire or need. Sixteen years of public education, beginning at age five and ending at age twenty-one, is a luxury offered in no other nation. Reform Five would abolish the compulsory aspect, yet retain the time span of available instruction funded by public taxation. By making all postelementary education a voluntary venture, publicly supported programs would be utilized only upon student-consumer demand.

Student Learning Certificates would tend to place responsibility directly on the student and parents for use of the school facilities because of their personal selection of programs. Peer pressure could reduce the crime rate in the schools because those enrolled would be there at their own choice. Destruction of property would reduce their opportunities to learn those things they had selected.

The cost of tax funded instruction, beyond that required for the students to master the three R's, would depend directly on the needs of students. Not all students would remain enrolled even in voluntary learning programs. But there would be no cost at all until the Student Learning Certificates were cashed in for enrollment.

There would be a thirteen year time span for students to use the Certificates, good for an eight year period of learning. Opportunities for publicly funded education would extend to age twenty-five years. Once the Student Learning Certificates are used up, no matter whether the pupils succeeded or failed to learn, the cost of all subsequent instruction would become a personal affair at individual cost.

Fiscal reform of publicly supported education through distribution of Student Learning Certificates will underwrite equal school opportunities for all who wish to enroll. No longer will the disparity between rich and poor districts exist.

This reform implies that those schools, either private or public, which cannot operate programs successfully in open competition with other schools, would then be forced to close their doors.

When students have completed the compulsory Foundation Program, demonstrating competence in the three R's, they are then free to determine their own individual choices for all further tax supported education. Thus, it is in this context that the real significance of Student Learning Certificates becomes most evident to both the system and the student-consumer. But society, as a whole, stands to gain much in the long run!

Students not meeting sixth grade competency in the three R's would be required to use their Learning Certificate for remedial work. No longer would the taxpayer be required to pick up the tab for students who refused to work and learn during the Foundation Program of education.

Reform of school financing will require legislation which will make possible all school funding through statewide distribution of Student Learning Certificates, to provide each person with at least six years of opportunities for voluntary postelementary education.

Reform of state school finances must be integrated carefully, by established laws of reciprocity, with the concept of federal aid to education under the edict of equal opportunity for all youth, regardless of race, creed, sex, or place of residence.

Revision of school finances must establish funds sufficient to support educational programs for the total school population during the six-year period of voluntary student use. Reduction of annual expenditures from nonused certificates should be placed into an educational trust fund for subsequent draw by those who re-enter tax-supported instructional programs.

Success of the revision in school financing should be assessed at three year intervals to permit resolution of problems growing out of youth migration from school to school, district to district, and state to state.

17

Freedom to Learn

Perhaps the most convincing evidence that American secondary education needs a drastic overhaul is the current delinquency rate affecting, in one way or another, the lives of millions of boys and girls. High schools have become breeding grounds for crime and vice. Many students seem to have thrown off the entire school learning process.

Conclusions of opinion polls indicate that the situation is an outgrowth of pure idleness, absence of challenge, and lack of control. The system and ill-prepared educators are blamed for inability to cope with unruly and disinterested students who enroll in meaningless minicourses, take driver training after possessing a license, shoot drugs in the restrooms, and pull switchblades in the halls.

The issue facing the schools is really unrelated either to the causes or proportion of students involved in misconduct. The issue is automatic diplomas. Going to, remaining in, and graduating from high school has become expected and traditional. A common practice for business and industry is to employ only those students who possess a high school diploma. But when graduation becomes guaranteed as a right, regardless of competency, many a student cannot demonstrate the knowledge required to survive in even the most unimportant job. More than ever, entrance into the labor market depends upon demonstrable and salable skills often gained in activities unrelated to traditional school curricula.

Academic subjects as now taught may be learned easily by relatively few students. Others are able to gain certain skills more often than not from nonacceptable methods of teaching and extraschool activities. For large numbers of students, textbook instruction is the most artificial and ineffective means to learn anything.

Learning is difficult for some, easy for others. Most people learn best when they are motivated by the means most suitable to them. Very little motivation can be generated by educators when they require all students to be subjected to a compromised process geared solely to produce skills necessary for college entrance.

An effective means exists by which the majority of students can be taught. It is called "instilling the desire to learn." That is the basic mission of every teacher. It may be accomplished best by showing that learning makes a difference in personal lives.

Acceptable motivation can be identified immediately with economic gain and social status which awaits those free to select courses in which they can master the skills required for desired employment. This primary principle applies as well to those students whose ultimate job requires college training. All education relates, in one way or another, to some form of career development.

Reform must permit the schools to meet social demands. In time past, education was important because the educated were assured economic reward and social acceptance. Students, bombarded with counseling, parental, and peer pressures, were convinced that education was the "open sesame" to security and status.

People are once again demanding school reform to make educational programs economically worthwhile. For some, the process must be returned to the academic base; others insist courses must be geared to the preparation for a career. The two may provide one and the same foundation for learning.

Historically, the academic heritage of the high schools, up to the first quarter of this century, rested on vocational career goals. Students generally prepared to enter professions dependent upon graduation from high school and college. Most intended to become teachers, ministers, lawyers, or doctors. Today, students may look forward to entering hundreds of other occupations born of modern technology. The emphasis on career-related instruction still ranks uppermost in the public view.

The problem of school reform at the secondary level is one of organizing an effective balance in the curriculum. It is just as important for one student to be able to learn the skills necessary to become a successful welder, if that is his personal choice, as it is for another to select an academic course that will end in a law degree. Each may fulfill an individual ambition; both are required by society.

Every student must be given freedom of choice to select a program combining the essential elements of academic and occupational instruction necessary for each to reach his or her career goal. This is the basis of reform calling for *voluntary* programs in career development at the secondary level.

The secondary school curriculum, so long divided into academic and vocational divisions, will now come to an end. Educators will be unable to force the lower one-third of the pupil intelligence group into the so-called general programs. Specific courses will remain in the curriculum only so long as they meet student demand.

Paynter Plan Reform Six

Organize each high school attendance area into a Career Development Complex to provide all students who have demonstrated competency in the three R's with up to eight years of voluntary programs in career oriented instruction in response to student-consumer demand.

The reorganization of each high school attendance area into a Career Development Complex could be carried out with relatively few revisions. Only limited changes would be required; each would be permissive in nature. Reorganization of secondary education depends first upon public acceptance of educational reform.

Turning the current high school process from a compulsory into a voluntary concept will require legislation to be coordinated between the state and national governments. The Career Development Complex will operate on public funds disbursed only through Student Learning Certificates. Responsibility will be in the hands of all people served by the school process. The accountability for quality programs, coming under the authority of the district board of education, can easily be measured by the public.

The Career Development Complex will be evaluated by student latitude in the use of the state-funded Learning Certificates. Broadscale enrollment in specific programs offered at particular facilities indicates active and vitalized student approval.

Every Complex will operate with six divisions including:

1. Student Enrollment Index
2. Student Performance Index
3. Administrative Operational Index
4. Staff Performance Index

5. Program Effectiveness Index
6. Budget Control Index

For the first time in American history, the goal of elementary instruction will be harmonized to meet state and national concerns. Students who master acceptable levels of performance in the three R's enter the tax-supported Career Development Complex by choice. No longer will the secondary school function center on an extended review of the elementary curricular offerings. A new base will be built for *voluntary* learning of those skills to meet students' own individually determined goals. Student choice and student success provide the foundation for public evaluation of the educational process.

The administrative organization of the Career Development Complex, under the direct legal control of the district board of education, will follow traditional patterns, usually determined by specific functions. For example, each district would retain the office of superintendent, the function of which would be to execute all programs. The superintendent, as the management arm of the locally elected board, would be supported by administrative assistants who make the system operational. But direct management would rest with the director of the Career Development Complex, who will administer the reform in secondary education.

The director would be responsible for the complete operation of all facilities within the complex. He or she will be a new breed of educator, offering control in the support services to carry out successful programs. Employment of all instructional staff would be a major function of the director.

The secondary education will be composed of an integrated six-year span of learning. If the separate Junior High School concept is utilized, it will operate as an integral wing of the multifacilities within the overall Career Development Complex. The principal-coordinator of each educational component is responsible to the Career Development Complex director for carrying out all support services necessary.

In no way does the Community Education Council control the Career Development Complex. Elected members of the council will be involved with the district board of education to provide avenues of effective coordination between the compulsory Foundation Program and the voluntary programs offered at the secondary level in each Career Development Complex. The Complex possesses the latitude to provide students with a college-bound curriculum if that should be the students' choice.

Student-Consumer Demands

Students may attend a college; they may opt to be trained by industry. They may enroll in an approved private institution, or they may decide not to attend any particular school. They might even elect to join the National Youth Corps and leave the community area; they might choose to go to work in some terminal type job before returning to school, since Learning Certificates are valid for a thirteen-year period.

The instructional program in each Career Development Complex will be no better than its ability to draw and hold the student enrollment. Under the voluntary concept, evaluation of district, Complex, and teaching effort will be evident. Constant upgrading of programs will be the very lifeblood of every Complex. Standards by which to measure success will rest on the programs and methods that encourage students to enroll.

Programs will embody a professional pursuit of excellence. Student, parent, and staff commitment must revolve around instructional improvement. Achievement of purpose will depend solely upon meeting the demands of students who decide to expend their certificates at a particular Complex. Education, offered to meet student-consumer demand, will eliminate state compulsory attendance laws and

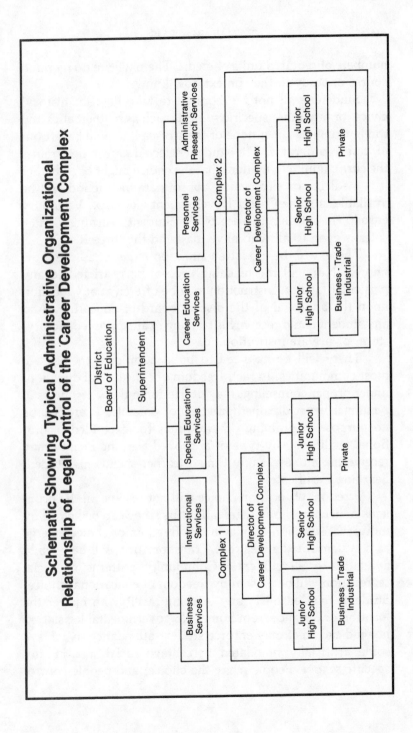

Schematic Showing Typical Administrative Organizational
Relationship of Legal Control of the Career Development Complex

numbers of required units of credit. There will be no *required* course of study in the context now known.

Students will not be required to take English, history, civics, or any other specific subject, such as mathematics and foreign language. Yet none of these disciplines will be left out of career programs. The student-selected career determines the curriculum. No matter what the choice might be, whether it is medicine or electronics, appropriate instruction will be available at some Career Development Complex. Voluntary enrollment through the use of the Student Learning Certificates is open to all who have mastered the three R's.

There will be no attendance boundaries as are now known. Nor will the teaching process be restricted to any particular facility. Instruction may be offered at any location upon the approval of the district board of education. And any student could receive his training in an approved factory, store, or private institution.

There will be no need to build additional facilities in most communities. In fact, freedom of educational direction, under proper counseling, may utilize community resources in a manner never dreamed practical or possible. There will be no purpose in draining off tax funds for expanded institutional facilities. Any type of approved learning facility may receive tax money at any time a learner spends his Student Learning Certificate.

Freedom of location choice will not resolve all the problems of neighborhood segregation. But they can be helped by individual selection. Nor will this freedom of choice emerge as a system for the wealthy. Transportation will be equally available to all students. Community patterns of racial segregation will be broken by freedom of educational choice. Students may enroll in any learning facility, no matter the location or distance from home. No governmental legislation nor judicial edict may enforce student attendance to achieve some artificially mandated percentage racial mix in any specific school. People make the choice; and people control the quality of instruction. This is the workable answer to the national concern over forced busing.

18

Name Your Goal

A major reform of the Career Development Complex will be in curricular programs. Instruction offered to voluntary students must be developed from a new philosophy. Courses must provide fusion of knowledge and skills.

Paynter Plan Reform Seven

Organize a voluntary, six-year program of studies for the Career Development Complex to implement skill development courses. Each course is to be designed by community, business, vocational, and professional leaders working in concert with educators to provide learning necessary to meet the individually selected occupational goals.

No longer will courses themselves be required as such; they will constitute a process by which students may reach a goal. The infusion of career education into the total instructional program combines all subject matter, including the

177

academic, technical, and vocational areas. The Career Development Complex will provide the bridge between course credit requirements and individually selected instructional units leading to actual work. The attitude that career education is only for the few will end. All education offered to postelementary students will be employment oriented for immediate or delayed entry into the work world.

One major objective of the Career Development Complex will be the upgrading and expansion of occupational education. When career instruction is part of the traditional academic approach, all qualified students will receive a significant education. Under the voluntary enrollment process, by expenditure of the Student Learning Certificates, each who wishes to do so may leave school armed with employment skills, whether or not he ever plans to pursue further education in a technical school or college.

Most students today enroll in courses because they are required for the next step in the educational ladder reaching upward toward nothingness. The result has been that most students defer making their career decisions until the schooling process is completed. Many fail to prepare for anything. Increasing numbers do not achieve even the basic educational requirements to attain literacy.

The tragedy of secondary programs is no more evident than in the vital statistics which reflect a national horror. Only twenty percent of all jobs listed in the *Department of Labor Index* require college training. Yet, eighty percent of the current high school student body are enrolled in general education or college prep programs. Neither prepares students to make the transition from school to the employment market. The imbalance between educational need and the existent study programs provides a major impetus for curricular reform.

No specifically required courses are demanded of students enrolled in the Career Development Complex. They are not required to "sit through" history, civics, mathematics, or

English. Yet none of these courses are left out of the program! Once the student goal has been determined, he will be guided into a planned set of courses, developed like building blocks by those actually practicing the particular career sought.

Every student enrolled in the Career Development Complex will be guided through courses leading to his or her individually selected career goal. Urban students, no less than their rural counterparts, must understand the learning requirements of a physician, a lawyer, an engineer, an electronics assembler, or a day laborer in a factory. Students must be shown the relationship of particular courses in science, mathematics, history, and English, and how each is integrated in the program of skill development units. All are essential equipment for later entry into a particular career. Successful completion of any part or the entire six-year educational experiences at the Career Development Complex would enable the student to enter either the labor market or take the next step to further required schooling.

The architects of the curriculum will be those who actually practice each particular career. Local committees of technical "experts" will meet with curriculum specialists to design courses of learning. Representatives of the Bar Association will determine courses necessary for a student to become a lawyer. The entire spectrum of courses would be listed, along with an appropriate explanation for each. Those who seek to enter the professions will follow a set of course requirements in preparation for college entrance. Each particular goal would be composed of courses, determined by college admissions officers, leading to successful entry into higher education.

Farmers would participate in planning the courses for that vocation. If a student selected news reporting as a career goal, he would be guided through a personalized curriculum. In this case, the main emphasis would be on English grammer and composition, as well as actual practices to enhance related skills of inquiry, documentation, organization, and reporting. Courses necessary to train a student to become an

A Glance At One Poll's Adult Ratings of Public School Experiences

1. More than seventy-five percent remembered a lack of adequate educational and career guidance. Adults interviewed cited a lack of knowledge of their own interests and abilities, related to educational and occupational opportunities. Most pointed out wasted time, decline in motivation, and personal frustration because they learned too late that a work-oriented society awaited them.

2. A vast majority reported uneven quality of teaching. Well over half of those responding cited widespread negative methods and attitudes in their teachers. More than a few remembered and appreciated teachers who encouraged student interest in literature, science, math, and history by exhibiting competence, showing personal preparation, and being hard taskmasters. Many expressed bitter memories of teachers who were disrespectful to students. Most demanded that the oversupply of teachers be utilized to replace incompetent instructors who were employed under tenure laws or just for the salary.

3. Two-thirds believed their education would have been improved by individualizing the instructional methods. Nearly eighty percent believed the system should have enlarged student choice of interesting courses. A huge majority wanted more training in the academic subjects, but alongside career instruction.

4. Many considered the entire counseling process an outright failure. Most cited the academic-oriented counselor as inappropriately trained to handle personal attention to out-of-school problems. All believed the guidance function was geared solely for the college prep students.

5. Nationally renowned educators conclude that schools have shortchanged those students who need the services the most. School success has been most evident with those students who were successful in college. The most bitter indictment of the system centered on absolute failure of schools to develop curiosity in the social areas of justice, individual rights, the political processes, and economic freedom within the historical heritage of the nation.

auto mechanic would be determined by those trained in the field.

In each case, no matter the job, career, or college goal, the course content would be determined by those active in the field. No longer would educators enjoy despotic control over curricular requirements. Professional educators would have to develop the best methods in the art of education for approval and adoption by their district boards of education.

The impact of career development experiences on news reporting may just as well be equally appropriate for the traditional subject matter in science, history, or foreign language. Career education will be a process by which all instruction is blended into an individualized curriculum. No longer will students be forced to progress through a system of academics, general or vocational. But the real impact becomes evident when the public understands that career development provides preparation for the entire spectrum of jobs, including college preparation for the professions.

1. Students leaving the Career Development Complex will have learned salable skills required to enter and be successful in identified jobs.

2. Students completing the secondary phase of instruction will have attained a competence sufficient to continue into further preparation at the next higher educational institution.

3. Students are provided actual placement services as the culmination of the studies offered at the Career Development Complex.

Individually selected career goals may be identified within the fifteen career clusters, representative of more than 45,000 separate jobs, as developed by the U.S. Office of Education:

1. Business and Office
2. Marketing
3. Communications Media
4. Construction
5. Manufacturing
6. Transportation
7. Agribusiness
8. Marine Science
9. Environmental Control
10. Public Services
11. Health
12. Hospitality and Recreation
13. Personal Services
14. Fine Arts and Humanities
15. Consumer and Homemaking

Each Career Development Complex may select all or only specific clusters to underwrite the program to meet local needs and demands. The alternative would be to specialize in selected areas offering students a particularly outstanding program. Each cluster includes jobs at all levels of preparation and skill development, from an entry level bus boy through the skilled trade of carpenter. But each also covers technical, paraprofessional, and professional careers.

The unique contribution to educational reform of the Career Development Complex is based on a complete break from traditional organizational structure. Valid freedom of educational direction is dependent upon this curricular reform.

19

Help Always
at Hand

      The purpose of the guidance program, basic to the operation of the Career Development Complex, will be to help students determine career choices. Specially trained counselors from every level of learning, occupation, and profession will provide continuous service.

      Although school guidance services have been provided for nearly fifty years, specialized counseling is considered to be one of the newer aspects of public education. The modern citizen feels education for his children is an individual matter. In many ways that attitude is commendable, yet it is one of the major causes for current public controversy. Most criticism of the modern school centers around curriculum, teaching methods, and teachers' evaluation of the student. The real tragedy is the inadequate program of individualized counseling to help choose the education best for and most desired by each student.

      Teachers are committed to participate in helping individual students succeed. Guidance and teaching are related. But guidance and counseling are very different concepts.

Traditionally, guidance was vocational. For many schools, guidance still means nothing more than placing students in jobs whenever they choose to leave school. Guidance efforts are thought necessary only at the secondary level. At the present time, the high school is still the major employer of guidance personnel.

Guidance is often pictured as a paternalistic process existing to mold students into desired social groups. Most group testing, to determine intelligence levels or interests, is administered in guidance programs. Out of this has come protests from parents and students that group guidance and mass testing makes students nothing more than computerized statistics without personal identity.

The group process in the guidance program is usually carried out by members of the teaching staff who act as student advisers. Students are assigned to a particular teacher-adviser by alphabet, homeroom, or subject matter. The number of students assigned to any one adviser varies and shifts are made upon student request. Within this group guidance process, the distinction between academic and personal problems becomes evident. The former is considered the province of teacher-advisers using group techniques; the latter opens the door for students to request specialized counselors.

The counseling process has evolved rapidly since 1930, when it emerged full-fledged to provide every student with a personalized "school resource person" who would offer direction, or referral services, if professional diagnostic or clinical help were required. The counselor's task is to help the parent/ student determine realistic goals. This done, both the counselor and the student can focus attention on an individualized program of studies for achievement of this goal.

The success of student counseling depends upon the practices used. As the process has developed, counseling may be considered as a face-to-face period in which, by reason of training, skill, and confidence vested, one person helps another person resolve pertinent personal problems.

Paynter Plan Reform Eight

Provide each parent/student with licensed counseling, payable by Learning Certificate stubs valued at a fixed sum per semester for professional services, computed at a determined figure per half hour, to be rendered upon request at any time convenient to the consumer.

Valid reform of the counseling process means the counselor will be removed from the actual school scene. He or she cannot be assigned a given number of students. The services must be available, upon demand or referral, to any student who seeks advice, direction, or help about any problem that impedes the progress toward personal, educational, or career goals.

The off-campus counselor will remain free from any disciplinary referral. He or she will be free to seek diagnosis and, if necessary, retain clinical and psychological services to aid in counseling. The counselor's goal will be to help the student develop maturely and, if necessary, to rehabilitate through close cooperation with the home, teachers, and any community agency.

Since all counseling will be related to, but totally removed from, the Career Development Complex, facilities will be used only for learning. Professional counseling cannot be effective when it must be fitted between classes or during a study period. All counselors will maintain their offices in Community Education Centers. Their services will be available to every student, beginning at the midpoint of the sixth grade and continuing throughout the six-year span of enrollment in the Career Development Complex.

School guidance programs, on the other hand, will remain on campus under the direction of teacher advisers. This kind of advice requires only friendly, intelligent interest.

For counseling service, students will be able to use special stubs on their Student Learning Certificates, equivalent, for example, to $200 per semester, computed at $20 per half hour. The counseling services are placed on the open market; the salary of the counselor is fixed by the case load he or she wishes to handle.

The fees, paid by certificate, cover both counselor preparation and interview time. The schools will be required to provide student records. School time missed for counseling interviews will be considered as any medical appointment. Use of off-school hours, evenings, and Saturdays will be encouraged.

The parent/student selection of a counselor depends on personal choice. If someone wants a black counselor, a religious counselor, or a medical counselor, each will be available, as long as he is licensed to render services at the Community Education Center. If, by chance, there is a personality clash, another counselor will be available, but at additional payment of another certificate stub. The choice is not restricted to a particular Community Education Center. The freedom of choice is limited only by the personal decision regarding the expenditure of the certificate stub. Additional counseling time over and above the $200 per semester may be purchased by the student-parent and is not an added burden to the taxpayer. Special handling of drug problems is a reality and a patient-doctor relationship is available.

Each counselor will possess a course of study manual, with descriptions and requirements to attain specified goals. A similar manual containing a complete profile on each teacher will be available. The counselor will lay out the potential courses, explain the content and the relationship of each, and indicate the entire pattern of preparation necessary to meet the student-consumer's goal.

Before he decides to spend his certificates, the student will know exactly what can be learned, the qualifications of the instructor, and the cost of the courses. For the first time in public education, each student will have access to teacher and curriculum profiles. With the advice of a professional counselor, the various pieces of each personal educational picture can be fitted together to meet the individual student's needs.

20

Fiscal Planning — Finally

While public attention may be mainly on the spiraling cost of national governmental operations, the ever mushrooming expenditures of state and local governments also raises the ire of taxpayers. Many a wild scheme comes from state legislatures and the tax-setting authorities, the local school boards. It would appear both groups of elected officials regard governmental programs as a type of growth industry. The demand for new programs requires constantly increased taxation. Oppressive taxation has become a reality, and no tax is more evident to the public than that imposed upon property to support the operation of public schools.

When people expect action to streamline school operations, boards continue to retain costly practices. In some cases, outmoded programs are set in motion. One means of returning school control to the citizens is to fund the local district by an actual count of Student Learning Certificates expended by those who voluntarily attend classes.

In 1928, just over 3.5 percent of the national income was spent for public education. By 1950, this had fallen to 2.9 percent, and the 1976 budget indicates a national expenditure of only 2.0 percent. Public education, while costing more dollars, is dependent upon a smaller portion of the national wealth.

The source of funds is only one element of public education's financial problems. Equal educational opportunities, based on equitable allocation of school tax funds, is an even greater problem.

During recent years, most states have attempted to develop funding based on formulas for state guarantee of funds. The state applies a politically conceived and controlled formula to determine necessary tax revenues to be apportioned to each school district. The fundamental purpose is to calculate the minimum amount of money required by each district annually to operate a basic school program. The political formula is then applied uniformly to all districts in the state.

The effort to ensure a minimum school budget is usually based on Average Daily Attendance (ADA). The local systems are encouraged to supplement their funds with additional taxation. Equal educational opportunities, based on equitable allocation for programs, go out the window. Wealthy communities can easily vote supplemental funds, but poverty areas often cannot offer more than minimally funded programs.

The American school system is filled with contradictions. The number of people to be educated is not necessarily related to the sources of the wealth that can provide sound programs. In general, the areas with the largest number of students are lowest in per capita ability to pay. School district income, based on distribution by political formulas, will no longer do. Adequate support for schools, founded upon a revolutionary source of funds, will achieve equality of allocation of revenue.

The U.S. Supreme Court decision on *Serrano v. Priest*, requiring equal educational opportunities for all students by statewide equity of funding, is a judicial mandate. Most educators hailed the decision as the basis for fiscal reform, in which money from wealthy districts would be allocated to poor areas.

A Glance at Taxing Inequity

1.   Beverly Hills, California, had an assessed valuation per average daily attendance of $58,992 from which school revenues could be generated by local taxation.

   a.   Only 7.2 percent of the students were listed as members of minority groups.

   b.   Only 5.2 percent of the students were listed as children from poverty level families.

2.   Baldwin Park, California, had an assessed valuation per average daily attendance of $5,474 from which school revenues could be generated by local taxation.

   a.   44.6 percent of the students were classified as members of minority groups.

   b.   13.2 percent of the students were listed as children from poverty level families.

Paynter Plan Reform Nine

Establish an Educational Finance Index to make it possible for the states to predetermine an accurate cost basis per course unit, so that instructional effectiveness may be evaluated through public accounting of all school expenditures.

Public education can avoid eventual bankruptcy by ascertaining school funding needs with the Educational Finance Index. This reform will make it possible for legislators to predetermine an accurate cost basis per course, rather than basing costs on attendance. Statewide teaching effectiveness will also be subject to evaluation through public accounting of all school expenditures of monies gained from Student Learning Certificates. Not only will school costs be determined, but educational priorities can be established. The Index will reveal both costs and results of spending.

The actual mechanics to implement this reform are simple. After determination of the administrative expenses for the Community Education Center, required funding for the Foundation Program is computed on a per classroom cost basis. The state provides directly to the district all funds necessary to educate every student in programs equally in every school district. Each postelementary student may apply for and receive from the state—but distributed through the Community Education Center—a Learning Certificate, to be cashed only upon enrollment at any approved institution.

Coupons affixed to the Student Learning Certificate provide the funds required for enrollment in a career development course. After administrative expenses have been determined for the overall operation of the Career Development Complex, the state provides equal funds, on a per course cost basis, directly to each student who may enroll by cashing the certificate.

The individual controls the use of the certificate. If utilized for enrollment, the institution selected receives the funds; if uncashed by the student, no public money is expended. District or state audit will then reveal an accurate accounting of educational expenditures on a per course cost basis. The exact costs of publicly funded education will be known.

The Student Learning Certificate will be devised with detachable coupons, each valued at a fixed amount per individual course cost. For example, a coupon will be worth the actual cost for instruction less only those predetermined administration, transportation, health, and capital outlay expenditures.

A further illustration might clarify the mechanics of this reform. If, for example, the total value of a certificate for an entire year at the junior high school level was fixed at $2200, the separate coupons would be variable in value to meet the different costs of individual courses. In like manner, the total value of the certificate for an entire year at the senior high school level might be fixed at $2500, and the figure fixed as high as $3000 for an entire year at the community college level. In any case, the value of each separate coupon would also be variable to meet the different costs of individual courses.

The Educational Finance Index is a reform by which actual instruction costs will be predetermined. It is a means of saying that the provision of each student with a given amount of education costs so much. Legislative support for public education must be based on such an index.

21

Committee
Called to Account

Traditional methods of financing public education have not provided evaluation through public accounting by independent audit. The Educational Finance Index will be a legitimate system of cost and equal educational opportunity control. But it must be developed and overseen by a State Accounting Committee.

Paynter Plan Reform Ten

Establish a legally constituted State Educational Accounting Committee, comprised of eleven members representative of the legislature, state board of education, Community Educational Council, district board of education, regional administrative unit, business, industry, professional administrators, tenured teachers, and classified school employees, to review educational expenditures audited by an independent firm. The Committee's express purpose is to develop an Education

Finance Index by which all school costs will be determined.

A State Education Accounting Committee would be made up of the following members:

1. One state senator

2. One state assemblyman

3. One state board of education member

4. One business representative

5. One industry representative

6. One Community Education Council representative

7. One district board of education representative

8. One regional administrative unit representative

9. One professional administrator

10. One tenured teacher

11. One classified school employee

This public citizen's committee would work in concert with an independent auditing firm serving the committee in the capacity of an executive director. The State Educational Accounting Committee would develop an Education Finance Index to recommend a five-year cost plan, which would be affected only by inflationary or deflationary conditions. Spiraling educational costs will no longer be based solely upon expansion of programs and services desired.

Annual reports of course costs will be formulated by the various school districts and councils and submitted to the state department of education. These will be compiled into an overall statewide report for presentation to the State

Educational Accounting Committee for detailed review of the separate, yet total, course costs. From this analysis will come a public accounting of educational programs. The elimination or addition of courses or programs will be a local decision made following a determination of funding available. The major function of the State Educational Accounting Committee will be to recommend funding limits for the entire five-year period. The combining of costs for courses and programs required for a well-rounded educational experience makes a valid cost index.

The State Educational Accounting Committee will recommend the amount of funds to be made available. The committee may determine, for example, that the state should finance only five periods per student per day in the voluntary career courses. Administrators will then know that, over a five-year period, only the established amount of funds will be available. The state will apply annually the current cost of living index to established educational expenditures. The fourth year will bring a new cycle of study and a revised Education Finance Index, to be activated during the following year.

Additional compensatory funding for specialized programs will be determined by including such extra expenditure as a part of a state's obligation. This plan guarantees statewide equity of all programs supported by tax revenues and provides the means to eliminate local property tax increases. This is a method of school financing representative of the wishes and desires of the people at every level.

Help for the Legislature

The final responsibility of the State Educational Accounting Committee is to compile and present alternatives to the state legislature when it is considering any financing bills for public education. Funding alternatives will be based on the independent auditing firm's information relevant to the affect of and funding reduction or increase on instruction programs. The state legislature would then be responsible for adoption of the five year Educational Finance Index.

Since school districts would have continuous knowledge of available funds, local planning and redevelopment of district curriculum would be facilitated. School districts would be free of constant local pressures for "add on" programs. District planning can be undertaken for research and development of improved programs at lesser cost.

Cost of living increases in available state funding would be built into the process to permit districts to maintain a program of education which remains constant in value.

No longer will distribution of funds be inequitable. Each student will be guaranteed equal educational opportunities. Tax rate elections, which always divide people, neighborhoods, and communities, will be a gripe of the past.

The determination of school expenditures and the allocation of tax funds are presently established separately from any attempts to determine program costs for particular grades, classes, or courses. Little attention, other than "add on" dollars, has been given to courses requiring special, extra cost funding.

Tax money today may be defined as some lump sum provided and distributed by the state to the local districts, for further distribution to the separate schools, for yet an additional distribution to support particular programs. Funding priorities established by research and planning are unknown to most educators. Maximum and minimum costs have yet to become an actual part of educational financing procedures.

Classroom teachers have seldom had an active voice in planning educational budgets. Yet they have much expertise to offer in examining course costs. Instead, most instructors are required to teach courses within financial constraints determined by those furthest from the scene. Few builders of roads, bridges, or homes would even begin construction without first examining costs in minute detail.

This concept is foreign to planning educational needs. Teachers are simply assigned a course, allocated certain supplies, and told to teach. When funds are exhausted, teachers are expected to replan methods and use of materials on some make-do basis.

Generating funds for public education from local sources, such as the property tax, is a most archaic method of supporting equal school programs. It must be remembered that, wherever the tax power is delegated, it is always imposed under special restrictions. All states prescribe, by law or constitutional provision, some kind of limit to the amount of taxes which may be levied. Such limitations usually apply to the maximum rate applicable to assessed valuations of property. The effect of new or reduced limits placed on local property taxes forces the school district to operate on funds raised elsewhere, such as sales taxes, through a shift in either the sources or the levels of revenues.

Any decrease in local taxes only increases the state support for schools. Some educators believe that one sure means to eliminate local control of the schools would be to centralize all financial support at the state level. So long as local and state participation in the planning and determination of costs and expenditures is maintained through elected and appointed representatives, however, the public will retain an overall voice in the school funding process.

The only logical method of funding schools is one which places the burden on the state. Perhaps this will evolve into a plan where school revenues will be state-collected and locally shared. It has been assumed that the national government has no financial responsibility for public education. Federal aid is given in the form of block, or categorical, grants of money for specialized programs. All financial aid, derived from general taxes, is intended to equalize educational opportunity without undermining local control. This theory has been applied with equal force in the battle for state and local control of the schools. Consequently, federal funding for education is processed through the states for distribution to local districts.

If states are to be held responsible for funding public education, then each must establish the means to raise tax money for school support. Such taxation might be in the form of property, sales, and/or income taxes.

But whatever the sources may be, they should be established by law, not left for public referendum, which only locks in fixed amounts. Minimum levels of taxation then form the political base above which elected officials fear to go. Consequently, tax sources must remain under the legislative process. The determination of how much tax support must be established by the democratic process through the State Educational Accounting Committee.

22

Finance Index
Tells All

Today's district taxpayers have proclaimed
that they are no longer willing to provide education at the
levels demanded by educators. Community citizens have
drawn the line beyond which local boards of education must
not go. State legislators, too, issue the same cautions,
demanding valid measurement of programs that require extra
funding, and, indeed, all school expenditures.

When the right time arrives, the state will provide total
funding for public education. The determination of the support level will be established by legislative adoption of the
Educational Finance Index. It will determine the minimum
and the maximum amounts of school revenues. With
statewide allocation of tax funds, it then will become the
responsibility of the local district or Community Education
Council to provide the best possible program within the
known amount of financing.

Beyond the state provisions for grades, classes, or
courses, any variations must be met by individual parents. It
is time for the public to understand that the state cannot provide funds to educate every student who would become a

doctor, a professor, or a scientist. It is possible for the state to guarantee a maximum amount of funding for *equal* programs within every school district.

Paynter Plan Reform Eleven

Allocate state funds to local district Boards of Education or Community Councils on a predetermined and equal ratio for each student, based on an established Educational Finance Index adopted by legislative action.

Under this reform, the allocation and distribution of funds are provided after the amount—based upon the established Educational Finance Index—is determined for the individual student. These funds are to be applicable by grade or course level. Funds no longer will be generated by average daily attendance. No longer will ADA (Average Daily Attendance) play a major role in district income. All funds are provided on actual student enrollment in specific grades or courses.

Funds for the elementary Foundation Program will be established for each of the grades, and allocated on the basis of actual student enrollment to the local district for use by the Community Education Council. Funds required for district-wide operation, including administration, transportation, and maintenance, will be determined by the board of education of the district encompassing the several Community Education Centers. The district accepts the responsibility for wise spending and local accounting of all funds.

If, for instance, $2,000 is allocated for each student enrolled in a particular primary grade, the teacher knows that at least that amount of funds is available each year to educate every student in that class during a five-year period. Any additional funds could be counted on only in relationship to increases in the cost of living index. It is at this point that the teacher, with new professional responsibility, will control expenditure, deciding:

1. How the money is to be used.

2. What assistance is needed.

3. Additional training necessary.

4. Purchase of supporting books and supplies.

5. Field trips, films, or counseling services.

6. Teacher salary beyond established minimum schedules.

The expenditures for total classroom instruction effort will be controlled completely by the teacher. The contract to teach a particular grade or class will be evidence of professional commitment to account for the total learning program.

The teacher in the Foundation Program in each Community Education Center submits to the Community Education Council the proposed classroom plan. Upon approval, the funding becomes available to the teacher for disbursement through the established district purchasing and accounting procedures. No teacher can be forced to commence, continue, or complete the program without those funds.

This is a revolutionary interpretation of teacher and administrator contracts. The teacher is accountable, in the terms of the signed contract, for the results of his or her approved plan. The administrator in his or her contract is responsible for seeing that the teacher carries out the plan.

Allocation of state funds to the local school district boards of education will have a different impact on the voluntary secondary level programs of career instruction. The traditional high school program is based on a five-class instruction schedule. These classes are normally provided on a semester basis to meet the requirements of course credit.

Any student who wishes to enroll in more than the state funded five periods of instruction, under the Paynter Plan, would be required to pay costs of additional selected courses as a personal obligation.

State funds, to support career development programs, would be allocated on the basis of individual course costs determined by the Education Finance Index. Coupons affixed to the Student Learning Certificates would represent varied values to permit voluntary student enrollment in high cost courses. The normal allocation of funds, represented by the total certificate value, would be based on a five course schedule per semester. Thus, the student possesses complete control of course selection during any particular semester.

State funding for individual students is based on specific grade or course costs. Even though the process varies between the Foundation Program at the elementary level and the voluntary programs offered in each Career Development Complex, the basic principle of funding education remains the same. All state funds are provided on an equal basis per student to meet indexed course costs.

23

The State at Local Level

The public believes public education is provided to boys and girls to meet the legal obligation of each separate state. Intentionally or no, the Founding Fathers provided no Constitutional reference to a school program.

Local school districts, as legal entities, are created by the state, but the state retains the primary responsibility for public education. Local districts' boards of education have been delegated a secondary authority to carry out the actual operation, but in the name of the state. As a result, just as there are fifty states making up this nation, there are fifty educational systems.

In practice, the state has taken more and more control of the operation of the local systems, always to "correct" some operational lack in local operation.

Acceptable state control of education depends upon partnership with the local school district operational authority. Both are necessary to worthwhile education; both are required to meet the federal principle outlined in the Constitution.

The political strength of any state depends upon its control over its multischool units without removing the delegated authority from the local communities. Should the state exercise total control, then it must also assume complete responsibility for the product. Few state legislators desire to do so. Therefore, local authority for school operation should be strengthened.

Paynter Plan Reform Twelve

Reorganize the administrative structure of the public schools by providing for additional political participation at the state level of community councils, district boards, regional units, and state board of education.

The political reorganization of the public school system would create an administrative structure composed of each of the following levels:

1. *Local Community*

Community Education Council members exercise the legal voice in school operation of the Community Education Centers which provide the foundation program of education.

2. *Separate School Districts*

Boards of education provide the legal control over all physical plants, budget accounting, and auditing responsibilities for the operation of the school district, encompassing at least one Community Education Center and Career Development Complex.

3. Regional Administrative Units

Regional Administrative Units, replacing County Offices of Education, provide legal control over the appeals procedure for students, staff members, and parents; the operation of community colleges; and all adult educational activities to carry out programs approved by the state board of education.

4. State Office of Public Instruction

The state board of education, directed by an appointed state superintendent, is legally responsible for meeting the needs expressed by the democratic voice in the state legislature.

A truly functional administrative office providing statewide democratic representation is almost nonexistent. Reform of the separate legal entities involved in school operation and control must be established. Most leaders agree that local boards of education should not be entrusted with the total control of their schools because the students are far more than community residents. They are really citizens of the region, state, and nation. Schools can never be permitted to operate under the total authority of any group of local people. At each level of administration, the basic school structure must represent distinct, but interrelated, social components. All must be granted the right to representation in legislative directives for the schools.

The Community Education Council provides the first-line control over the Foundation Program of the three R's offered in each Community Education Center. The Community Education Council is the voice of the local community. Legal control of the local school program is vested in elected representatives to the Council.

The district board of education is responsible for administering the logistics and fiduciary affairs of the Community Education Centers within the Career Development Complex.

The district board must provide the legal supervision of all physical plants, budget accounting of equipment and supplies, and maintenance of all facilities utilized by each Center and Complex within the district area. Candidates for membership on the board of education are elected to office by those serving on the several Community Education Councils. This political structure provides a direct relationship between elected community representatives to the Council and those exercising a representative voice on the district board of education.

Certain operational controls at the Career Development Complex will be relinquished by the board of education and granted to the individual student and parent, who will exercise their personal selection of the student's educational program and the courses to be taken.

The district board is responsible for appointing a superintendent, who is charged with coordination of the activities of the Career Development Complex. Much of the traditional operational authority of the superintendent will be vested in the director of each Career Development Complex. Employment of personnel is one of the legal responsibilities of the board. Personnel matters are resolved by the board through recommendations of the administrative staff.

Fundamental to any reorganization of the state system is the equalization of educational opportunities for all boys and girls. Intermediate units of administration, offices operating between the state department of education and the local district boards of education, will be dedicated to this. They will be called Regional Education Units. They will not decrease the administrative functions of local districts, but will provide an increase in necessary services. They will decentralize the state department of education.

Regional Education Units, designed to eliminate the traditional county offices of education, will operate under a regional board of education comprised of nine members elected at large by the qualified voters of the region. The elected board has a direct responsibility for funding and supervision of quality instruction throughout the schools within the entire region, with particular emphasis on adult education and community college programs. It must be responsive to the wishes of the people.

The Regional Unit serves as a resource center for study, research, and planning of long-range programs and procedures. Taking direction from the state department of education, it carries out a major burden of administrative leadership by providing research and program outlines. The unit is in a unique position: it will produce many support services to each of the respective districts within its boundaries. It serves as a clearing house for all forms of necessary research.

This research function is not to be construed as a statistics-gathering process. With essential research responsibilities, the unit will be as a separate arm in the statewide administrative structure. The pressures of collecting raw statistics must not undermine the research function. Valid research demands highly specialized personnel completely removed from both district operational activities and any political influence within the state board of education.

Study, review, and planning programs are additional functions of the staff at the Regional Unit. Each is necessary for coordination of the efforts by the separate districts to harmonize with a statewide educational improvement effort. Planning carried out at this level will involve the participation of many people, both inside and beyond the profession.

Perhaps the most visible function of the Regional Unit will be as an Appeals Board. This board will hear, evaluate, and recommend solutions to cases originating in either the several districts or the state department of education. Problem areas may be related to personnel or parental concerns. Recommendations could sustain the initial decision, or recommend resolution at the proper administrative level.

No matter the problem, actions taken by the Appeals Board will bring an end to buck passing on assignments, transfers, evaluation, sick leave and retirement, litigation filed by parents against the school districts, and measurement of instructional quality. This can relieve the courts of many a case, yet all parties remain free to take their complaints to a judicial court proceeding.

Constitutional provisions for public education vary from state to state, but nearly all include specific references to school finances, which shall be available to ensure that the educational program operates as a free statewide system. Many also embody sections on kinds of administrative organization. Many problems are created when the state provisions go beyond broad general statements fixing responsibility on the legislature to provide acceptable educational programs. When the state sets forth detailed prescriptions for educational control and operation, results tend to freeze such details into the code. Necessary revisions may take a difficult and time-consuming amendment process or the enactment of additional laws.

Many educators have lobbied for Constitutional protection of school support. They have attempted to stabilize educational programs, finance, and structure through specific code sections. The intent has been to entrap the legislature into fixed support levels. The results have often proved disastrous. The ultimate control has been firmly given into the hands of state lawmakers, and all segments of public education isolated from the actual decision-makng arena. Professional educators feel they must organize to petition governors and legislatures for laws which may permit educational revision.

This process has "watered down" valid input by public educators relating to the very programs they are later directed to implement. State lawmakers increasingly prescribe the details of finance, programs, administration, methods, and evaluation. They tend to reveal a legislative contempt for the competency of public school educators. To eliminate possible future centralized control of the schools, immediate reform is necessary.

The role of a state board of education will reflect the relationship between the legislature and the system of public education. If the superintendent of public instruction is appointed by the governor, the functions of the state board of education will be limited, for the superintendent must give primary support to the governor. Accountability for the administration of the school system by a popularly elected superintendent also fails to enlarge the role of a state board. Here, the superintendent is responsible directly to the voters. When legislatures enact specific detail into law, there is little power in the hands of the state board. It becomes a powerful office only when the lawmakers expand its administrative functions.

What is the most effective means to determine members of the state board of education? The Paynter Plan calls for a rotating fifteen member state board of education to be elected annually by a general caucus of the local district board of education and Community Education Council members. Each member elected to the state board will serve a four-year term in office; three members will be elected each year. To become eligible for election, a candidate must have served at least one term as an elected member of a particular Community Education Council, district board of education, or Regional Educational Unit.

The election of members by an annual caucus of the Community Education Councils and boards of education demands quality representation. The procedure creates an unusual opportunity for each Community Education Council and board of education to exercise a direct voice in the election of members who have served public education for a period of time. The state board will appoint the superintendent of public instruction, who will then be subject to confirmation by the upper house of the state legislature. Such ratification establishes specific status at the state level where political decisions determine the directions of public education.

The superintendent of public instruction can be considered the most important office in the educational system. It must be filled by a qualified professional educator. With vision, courage, and devotion to public education, the state superintendent can provide leadership for quality programs of instruction. Exemplary administration includes that of pointing out both the strengths and weaknesses of the system to legislators.

The strong political power base of the state superintendent is derived from ratification by the upper legislative chamber. But he or she must be required to devote full time to the office. The job will prohibit membership on any university or state college board of regents. The superintendent acts as the political arm of each community, providing leadership at the state level by working directly with school districts through the Regional Education Units.

The responsibility for the operation of public education, usually reserved to the legislature, would be limited to the funding areas. Lawmakers would establish minimum and maximum financing levels. But the instruction program would be left to state board policies, generated by the concerns of the Community Education Councils and the district boards of education. The responsibility to determine the quality of instruction and expenditure of funds would fall to the state board. It would determine limits within which the Community Education Center, the Career Development Complex, and the Regional Education Unit will function.

The successful operational control of public education means power felt at the state level. This can be accomplished *only* through effective involvement of local people serving in elective offices. They must elect the members of the state board of education, which, in turn, appoints the state superintendent. Ratification by the upper legislative house completes the cycle of educational control. The state superintendent becomes a "cabinet" level position.

Here is reform that provides an educational organization born of local control growing to district responsibility for efficiency, quality, and economy, through regional research, development, and appeal. The state board of education guides the system of public instruction with a voice that represents the feelings and desires of the local communities. Everyone, from the lowest level of involvement to the peak of political power, is part of this voice.

Afterword

Public education is the one focal point in all of the American society. Many kinds of schools comprise it. Private and parochial schools play their role, too. The fundamental theme, the twelve major reforms of the present system, will affect every educational institution.

Each reform is one component of total effort to improve the product. The premise for the Paynter Plan for Reform rests on the belief that education can be one of the most influential public institutions for good known to this nation. If the Paynter Plan is followed, the schools of the twenty-first century will insure students of instruction in the basic skills necessary to function as productive members of modern society. Additional learning will take place in voluntary programs at any approved facility selected by the student consumer.

Free, universal, and compulsory education is not necessarily equated with the most economical and productive system. Students now receive too much schooling, but not enough education. The author refuses to accept the assumption that all learning takes place in the schools.

No matter the location or type of institution, problems of student learning are common. But when students become bored and destructive of the school system, it is time to change.

Undoubtedly, a long period of institutional infighting during any transition will go on. Dramatic attacks from many elements will be played out. But when public education becomes a desired commodity, parents and taxpayers will want to support the total reform of public schools.

My twelve basic reforms are built on citizen involvement, from elected representatives at the local community level to state lawmakers. The "Big Brother" concept will be democratically refuted. The schools will be freed of government control. They will be back in the hands of the local communities where they physically exist.

Increased emphasis today on educational planning at the state and national levels makes it essential that the public understands what this means to local and regional participation. At this critical juncture, where planning meets politics, the public must become involved to help determine direction in their school systems, and to have a voice in that change.

The key people in our democracy are not business and political leaders. They are the professional educators employed by the schools of this nation. They shape the destiny of the community, the state, the nation. They are the men and women who mold the ideals and beliefs of future generations. The public can and must work with them to gain education that will fulfill its name for our youth and our nation.

Subject Index

Absenteeism, 163
Academic, 33
Academic achievement, 65
Academic program, 155
"Academy," 4
Accountability, 60, 73, 74,
  82, 130, 136, 145, 211
Accountable, 86, 138, 139,
  146
Achievement, 54, 90, 128,
  134, 138, 144, 157
Administration, 40, 59
Administrative structure, 206
Adult instruction, 29
Adult programs, 31, 33
Advancement, 30
Age requirements, 30, 91
Alaska, 24
Alcohol, 56, 163
Amendment to the Constitu-
  tion, Tenth, 23
America, 24
American colonies, 51
American Constitution, 47
American education, 14, 23
American Federation of
  Teachers, 73
American flag, 57
American Heritage, 66
American patriotism, 56
American public education,
  27
American schools, 52
Ann Landers, 12
Appeals Board, 209, 210
Arithmetic, 132
Athenian instruction, 50
Attendance, 163, 164
Attendance laws, 24, 87, 90
Audit, 192, 195
Australian, 57

Authority, 137, 144
Automatic diplomas, 167
Average Daily Attendance
  (ADA), 190, 202

Baldwin Park, California, 191
Bankruptcy, 191
Basic education, 129
Barnard, Henry, 20
Berkeley, 30
Beverly Hills, California, 191
Bible, 17
"Big Brother," 216
Board, 59
Boards of Education, 39, 40,
  60, 72, 144, 206
Boston Latin School, 31
Budget, 59, 146

California, 21, 74, 83, 87, 103
Career development, 181
Career Development Center,
  192
Career Development Complex,
  170, 171, 172, 174,
  178, 179, 181, 182, 183,
  185, 201, 204, 208, 212
Career development programs,
  204
Career education, 181
Career instruction, 178
Census Bureau figures, 162
"Certificate of Proficiency,"
  159
Certification, 25
Changes, 58, 59
Chicago's Community
  Christian Alternative
  Academy, 156
Child Labor Laws, 88
Chinese, 50

Church, 57
Citizenship, 54
City or independent district, 35
Civil Rights Act of 1871, 84
Civil Service, 72
Civilian Conservation Corps, 155
Collective bargaining, 83
College, 31, 169
  degree, 31
  expansion, 32
  Preparatory programs, 31, 44
  training, 151
Colonial, 19
  era, 19
  period, 19
  schools, 44
  settlers, 41
Columbus, 30
Commercial education, 52
Commitment, 147
Committee of Ten, 52
Common learnings, 152
Common school, 29
Common traditions, 37
Communications, 39
Community college, 31, 32
  councils, 202
  district, 35
Community Education Center, 120, 129, 131, 135, 137, 138, 139, 144, 146, 147, 151, 161, 185, 192, 202, 203, 206, 207, 212,
Community Education Council, 145, 147, 172, 201, 202, 203, 206, 207, 208, 211, 212
Community pressure, 82
Competency, 168
Compulsory attendance, 30, 87, 88, 90, 145, 152, 154, 155, 160, 172
  laws, 92, 157,
  education, 215
Concord, Vermont, 64
Connnecticut, 20
Consolidated district, 35
Constitution, 24, 56, 205

Constitutional, 205, 210
  Convention of 1787, 52
  rights, 85
Continental Congress, 20
Core Curriculum, 152
Corporal punishment, 26
Counseling, 168, 174, 183, 185
  services, 84, 186
Counselor, 183, 186
County district, 35
County Offices of Education, 207, 208
Credibility, 139
Crime, 88, 163, 167
  and violence, 132
Criminal behavior, 82
Criticism, 63
Curricula, 44, 52, 70, 88
  revision, 55
Curriculum, 63, 64, 132, 137, 147, 169, 179, 183
  alternatives, 128

Daily Pilot, The, 12
Dalton, Massachusetts, 65
David, 47
Decentralization, 67
Decision-making rights, 40, 57
Declaration of Independence, 56
Delinquency, 167
Department of Labor Index, 178
Dewey, John, 52
Disciplinary measures, 85
Discipline, 80, 82, 83, 84, 130, 132, 137
Dishonesty, 163
Dismissal codes, 72
Disneyland, 13
District Board of Education, 39, 146, 207, 212
Distrust, 80
Doctrine of Fairness, 85
Dossier, 136
Dropouts, 89, 90, 156, 162, 163
Drug, 82, 186
  abuse, 81
  offenders, 83

Drugs, 56, 82, 84, 163, 167
Due process, 84, 85

Early Childhood, 29
  Education, 151
Economic attitude, 44
  considerations, 54
  fluctuations, 55
Economy, 44
Education, 24
Education Finance Index, 191,
  193, 195, 196, 198, 201,
  202, 204
*Education Policies Commis-
  sion Report of 1963*, 51
Educational Function, 66
Educational Opportunity, 33,
  159
Educational reform, 52, 170
Educators, 38, 60
Elementary, 29, 30, 31, 34,
  52, 84, 128, 136, 138,
  144
  curriculum, 52
Elementary education, 161
Elementary instruction, 130,
  154
Elementary level, 204
Elementary school, 131, 151
Enforcement, 86, 87
English, 32
Equal educational opportun-
  ities, 190
Equal Opportunity, 25
Equalization, 208
European school system, 52
Evaluated, 170
Evaluation, 54, 65, 69, 71,
  74, 76, 80, 127, 137, 135,
  145, 146, 147, 183
Evaluations, 130
Excellence, 172
Experimentation, 79
Expulsion, 85, 86
Extracurricular activity, 128

Fads, 128
Faith, 80
Federal aid, 46, 199
Federal grants, 47
Financial aid, 199
Financial support, 67

Fiscal reform, 191
Florida, 46
Foundation Program, 129,
  130, 131, 132, 134, 136,
  138, 139, 144, 145, 151,
  152, 161, 165, 172, 192,
  202, 203, 204, 207
Founding Fathers, 205
Freedom of choice, 169
Free education, 24
Free School Law, 25
Funding, 190, 197, 198, 200,
  202, 203
Funds, 197, 199, 204

General Court, 18
Germany, 154
Goals, 54, 56, 179
Goss vs. Lopez, 84
Grammar, 14
Grammar school, 29, 30
Greek, 31
Greek tongue, 32
Guidance, 183, 184
Gymnasium, 52

Harvard, 31, 32
Harvard Report of 1892, 30
Hawaii, 24
Hebrew Kingdom, 47
Higher education, 32
High school, 30, 52, 90,
  154, 161, 167, 169, 170,
  203
High School Certificate, 89
High school diploma, 31
High school education, 29
Home, 57
Hoosier Schoolmaster, 68
Hopkins, Mark, 68

Illinois, 87
Illiteracy, 132
Illiterates, 129
Immunity, 84
Incompetency, 26
In loco parentis, 26, 27, 84
Innovation, 64, 128
Irving, Washington, 68

Jefferson, Thomas, 20
Jesus, 13

Job Corps Conservation Corps, 155
Joint, Consolidated or Union districts, 34
Judeo-Christian, 50
Junior college, 30
Junior high, 29, 30
Junior high school, 171, 193
Juvenile delinquency, 81

Kalamazoo (Michigan) Case, 25
Kindergarten, 29, 31, 151

Labor market, 89
Lancaster, Pennsylvania, 35
Lancasterian system, 35
Latin, 31, 32
Laws of Reciprocity, 165
Learning Certificates, 172, 192
Learning objectives, 54
Lecture-Recitation Practice, 65
Legal rights, 86
Lexington, Massachusetts, 69
Literacy, 151
Living Bible, 11
Local board of education, 23, 201
Local districts, 34
Local districts board of education, 202, 205
Local school boards, 21
Local school district, 34, 205
Local school district boards of education, 203
Los Angeles, 30
Los Angeles Times, 11
Lyceum, 52

McGuffey Reader, 13
Mann, Horace, 20, 69, 154
Massachusetts, 18, 20, 24, 87
Massachusetts Bay Colony, 17
Mathematics, 14, 31
Measurable achievement, 145
Measurement, 132, 134
Methodology, 138
Middle Ages, 18

Ministry, 32
"Modern" education, 50
Moral turpitude, 26
Morrill Act of 1862, 32, 44
Motivation, 168
Mr. Chips, 68

National Committee of Ten, 1893, 154
National Committee on Reform of Secondary Education (Rose), 91
National Council of Five, 1905, 154
National Education Association, 73
National income, 189
National Youth Corps, 155, 156, 157, 172
New Jersey, 24
New York, 24, 25, 69, 73 86
New York City, 35
Normal school, 69
Northwest Ordinance of 1787, 20

Objective measurement, 55, 128
Objective standards, 75
Observation, 79
Occupational education, 178
Ohio, 81
Old Deluder Act, 18
"On-the-job" training, 155
Oregon Case, 25

Paynter Plan, 129, 144, 152, 160, 163, 170, 185, 191, 202, 204, 206, 211, 215
Pennsylvania, 25, 86
Performance, 135
Philosophy, 64
Philosophy of Education, 49
Physical disability, 26
Physical resources, 37
Plan, 6-3-3, 30
Plan, 8-4, 30
Police, 84
Police control, 83
Political control, 43
Political issues, 38

Politicians, 38
Post-Civil War era, 44
Post-Revolutionary War, 20
Postsecondary education, 32, 33
Preschool, 29, 31
Principals, 127, 144
Professional educators, 43, 59
Progress, 137
Progressive, 53
"Progressive" education, 50
Property damage, 87
Property tax, 45, 67, 197, 199
Protestant Revolution, 50
Public control, 67
Public education, 43, 49, 54, 58
Public instruction, 52
Public schools, 29, 57
Public school movement, 20
Puritans, 19, 26, 51
Purpose of education, 51

Quadrivium, 18

Read, 14, 132
Reading ability, 131
Reading, writing and arithmetic, 52, 55
  see also Three R's
Reform, 13, 67, 144, 145, 147, 160, 165, 168, 185, 192, 193, 207, 211, 213
Regional Administrative Units, 207
Regional Educational Units, 208, 211, 212
Regional Unit, 209
Remedial, 33
Remedial reading courses, 12
Report card, 139
Representatives, 57
Required attendance, 25
Research, 209
Responsible, 138, 144
Responsibilities, 144
Responsibility, 137, 144, 145, 170
Revision, 128
Romans, 50
Rules of Conduct, 86

Rural district, 34

Salt Lake City, 154
San Francisco State College, 65
Scholastic Aptitude Test (SAT), 11
School aims, 54
School board, 40, 41, 58, 59, 60
School board trustees, 14
School districts, 38, 46, 66, 198
School failures, 60
School finance, 86
School financing, 43
School funds, 67
School reform, 169
Schools' responsibility, 55
Secondary, 29, 30, 31, 32
Secondary education, 154, 171
Secondary schools, 34, 44, 51
Segmentation, 12
Senior high school, 193
"Serrano Case," 146
Serrano vs. Priest, 190
Sixteen Fourty-four (1644), 18
Sixteen Fourty-seven, (1647), 18
Sixth grade, 6, 134, 135, 136, 138, 151, 152, 157, 160, 161
Sixth grade competency, 165
Small school district system, 37
Smith Hughes Act of 1917, 44
Social demands, 168
Social factors, 145
Solomon, 47
Standardized test data, 135
Standards, 75, 130, 137
State Accounting Committee, 195
State Aid programs, 46
State and National government, 41
State Board of Education, 207, 211

State Code, 56, 75
State Constitution, 57
State Education Code, 21
State Educational Accounting
    Committee, 195, 196, 197,
    200
State funds, 203
State government, 43
State legislatures, 36
State support, 199
State Teachers College, 69
Status Quo, 38
Strategies For Change, 71
Strike, 83
Student behavior, 86
Student Learning Certificates,
    163, 165, 170, 174, 178,
    185, 186, 189, 192, 204
Student performance, 138,
    147
Stull-Rodda Bill, 74
Superintendent, 40, 58, 59,
    60, 211, 212
Supreme Court, 25, 84
Suspension, 85

Tax, 189, 200
    bases, 37
    funds, 87, 163, 174
Taxes, 20, 43, 199
Taxing, 191
Taxpayers, 49, 89, 161
Tax rate, 40, 198
Tax revenues, 197
Tax support, 24, 25
Tax-supported colleges, 32
Teacher evaluation, 73
Teacher responsibility, 82
Teacher training, 69, 70, 72
Teachers, 59
Teaching methods, 183
Technical education, 31

Tenure, 26, 72, 73
Theories, 79
Third grade, 133, 134, 135,
    136, 161
Three R's, 17, 49, 52, 53,
    54, 57, 76, 88, 128, 129,
    130, 131, 134, 135, 147,
    152, 154, 160, 161, 165,
    170, 171, 174, 207
Town council, 19
Town selection, 19
Town or township district,
    35
Trade, 31
Traditionalist, 53
Twentieth Century, 51

Unification, 38
Union or Joint District, 34
United States, 37
Unity, 38
Universal, 24
Unprofessional, 26
Urban district superin-
    tendent, 59
U.S. Supreme Court, 24, 190

Valid, 79
Vandalism, 87
Vice, 167
Violence, 81, 82, 87, 88
Vocational, 33
    education, 52

Werts, Willard, 11
*White House Conference
    Report of 1955*, 51
Winnetka, Illinois, 65
Wood Decision, 85
Wood vs. Strickland, 84
World War II, 45, 88, 154
Writing, 132